Alana Jelinek is AHRC creative fellow at the Museum of Archaeology and Anthropology, University of Cambridge.

THIS IS NOT ART

Activism and Other 'Not-Art'

Alana Jelinek

I.B.TAURIS
LONDON · NEW YORK

Published in 2013 by I.B.Tauris & Co Ltd; reprinted 2014
6 Salem Road, London W2 4BU
175 Fifth Avenue, New York NY 10010
www.ibtauris.com

Distributed in the United States and Canada Exclusively by Palgrave Macmillan
175 Fifth Avenue, New York NY 10010

ISBN: 978 1 84885 856 5 (HB)
978 1 84885 857 2 (PB)

A full CIP record for this book is available from the British Library
A full CIP record is available from the Library of Congress

Library of Congress Catalog Card Number: available

Printed and bound by CPI Group (UK) Ltd, Croydon, CR0 4YY

FSC
www.fsc.org
MIX
Paper from responsible sources
FSC® C013604

Table of Contents

Introduction 1

Part I: Setting the Scene

CHAPTER 1 Neoliberalism and the Artworld 17
CHAPTER 2 We Who Police the Definition and Value of Art 43

Part II: Artworld Orthodoxies

CHAPTER 3 Understanding Power 65
CHAPTER 4 The Art–Life Dichotomy 93

Part III: A Celebration of Art Practice

CHAPTER 5 The Disciplinarity of Art Practice 119
CHAPTER 6 In Conclusion 151

Notes 163
Index 183

With thanks to:

Funders and support:
Liza Thompson, I.B.Tauris; Arts & Humanities Research Council

Readers and critics:
Derek Matravers, Larne Abse Gogarty, Dominic Rahtz, Juliette Brown

Inspiration:
Jane Trowell and James Marriott of PLATFORM; Nicholas Thomas and Anita Herle of Museum of Archaeology and Anthropology, University of Cambridge; Sarah Jack

Introduction

This book has been written at a particular juncture in my quest as an artist to understand the definition and value of art. For a political person with a predilection for philosophical thinking, the definition and value of art are not givens. Between 2004 and 2008, at Oxford Brookes University, I wrote a doctoral thesis that addressed this area. The starting point of that thesis largely reflected the stories prevalent within the artworld at the time. But two things have informed a change of heart that can be summarised as: 'I used to think I was an activist and then I met some'. This was the name of a talk I gave at the 2010 Association of Art Historians conference in Glasgow, on the invitation of Robin Baillie and Ken Neil, and its essence is the kernel of this book.

The activists I met in 2009 were PLATFORM as well as others involved in 'Climate Camp' and 'Art not Oil'. PLATFORM, an activist organisation creatively involved in raising awareness of the issues around fossil fuel exploitation, were asked to stage an exhibition to be held at the Arnolfini gallery, Bristol, in the lead-up to COP15 as part of the activist art season at Arnolfini. (COP15 was a gathering of world Heads of State and held in Copenhagen 2010 to determine policy addressing climate change and specifically rises in atmospheric CO_2.) In 2009, I was asked by Jane Trowell and James Marriott of PLATFORM, who had seen an exhibition I had curated in 1999 called 'empire and I', to work with them. My role was diplomatic rather than curatorial, creating bridges across the cultural divide of activism and the artworld, helping PLATFORM and the Arnolfini to communicate. This was a divide neither myself nor PLATFORM thought existed and yet it emerged in the two years before I was asked to help and the divide continued to be manifest throughout the exhibition process. In this role, I realised how 'artworld' were my assumptions, methodologies and knowledge base. However political I thought I was, I had to learn from scratch the assumptions and methodologies of activism.

Also in 2009, I began a Fellowship in the creative and performing arts funded by the Arts & Humanities Research Council (AHRC) at the Museum of Archaeology and Anthropology, University of Cambridge. This opportunity took me outside the artworld in another direction, to one that also had some engagement with contemporary art and the artworld from a similarly 'outside' perspective as became increasingly clear. Professor Nick Thomas and Dr Anita Herle, eminent anthropologists at the Museum, stage contemporary art exhibitions and invite contemporary artists to make interventions into the Museum, and it became apparent over time that they curated and understood art from their own disciplinary assumptions. Because my own education had been so multidisciplinary from the start – crossing practice and theory lines and institutions, going between art practice and academic disciplines (mostly philosophy and history, and philosophy of science) – I had failed to acknowledge the differences between both the various academic disciplines and between art and academia.[1] In encountering the disciplines of anthropology and archaeology for the first time, what struck me was both the similarities and differences between them and with art practice. Suddenly I understood *disciplinarity,* despite coming up against disciplinary boundaries for my entire professional life.

It is these experiences that have informed the ideas within this book. Rather than replicating assumptions about ethical or politicised art practice peddled by activists and the artworld alike, as I'd also done in my doctoral thesis 'Art as a Democratic Act', this book is an attempt at opening up those closed-down debates. I hope it will inspire others to consider art and art's social role in a new, more generative, light. At this moment in time, this is especially important both because of the ongoing, unchecked, ill effects of neoliberal systems and our inadvertent internalisation of its values, and also because of the perpetuation of moribund tropes within most contemporary art practices. Most contemporary art that claims a politics or ethics is so riddled with artistic and political cliché that it fails both as (interesting, innovative, important, ambitious) art and as effective activism, so that neoliberalism remains unchallenged as a form of totalising discourse. I will argue here about why art is important and why neoliberal values and systems undermine values that have been endemic to art practice throughout modernity. I will also argue that the capacity of art to speak of individual stories, agency and autonomy is particularly significant when faced with totalising narratives, including those promulgated and normalised at present within neoliberalism. Neoliberal values are widely reproduced in all aspects of mainstream culture, often casually and largely unwittingly, and I would feel like King Canute attempting to hold back the waves if it were not for the fact that a large section of the artworld claims to want to produce art of a radical political hue.

I have written this book in three parts, each with two chapters. The first part sets the scene. It describes the parameters of the book's investigation: namely, what art is and what is art's current context. The second part describes two lines within twentieth-century artworld debate that have led to a set of binaries. Though politically useful at the time, these binaries have produced, in the twenty-first century, a turgid set of rules that the artworld today blindly follows despite changes in political-social-economic context as well as an impotent nostalgia. The third part of the book answers the criticism described by the second and offers another way of understanding art practice, as a discipline, and its value within wider society.

The story of this book, in other words, is a story of art told for this time, this contemporary moment, in recognition of the preoccupations and history of radical art practices. It is told by an artist and from a doggedly London perspective, and so in no way do I wish to imply universality, be it geographical or historical. Running throughout this book is the conviction that geographic and temporal specificities matter, and that it is misleading and inaccurate to imagine that instances of (material) culture, like exhibitions or individual artworks, occurring in different cultures are understood in the same way in all cultures. The products of globalisation are experienced locally, through local preoccupations and histories.[2] This book aims to reflect accurately on the preoccupations of the contemporary London artworld, including a broad spectrum of professional practitioners, and our recent history.

In this book, I restate the stories that others have told, including those philosophers and theories oft-cited within the artworld; theories that, despite being cited over and again by curators, writers, critics and artists, seem to remain unheard or misconstrued. At any rate, though oft-repeated, they have had little effect on art as praxis. Most contemporary practice – including that claiming a politics, ethics or radicalism – maintains rather than undermines the status quo and particularly the neoliberal structures that privilege and enable the few over the many.

This book offers few examples of 'good' or 'political' or 'disruptive' art practices for a number of reasons. First, if we understand that power is fluid and so too is resistance, as will be argued, then all acts are time- and context-specific. They are contingent. Offering examples of best practice works in another register, *as if* there is one typology or mode of resistance, a universal. I wish to avoid creating yet more tropes of resistance to sit alongside those already in danger of ossification. There are clichés of resistance, like collaborative practice, or working with ephemera, or street art, or involving illegality, such as squatting or trespassing or fly-posting or graffiti. While it is true that these types of practice have been fruitful in producing interesting art, they have also been sites of tired cliché and sites where repressive or exclusive norms have been replicated. Just because something is done collaboratively, for example, doesn't mean it necessarily addresses fundamental issues of representation. Collaborative groups may also repress difference. They may replicate wider societal imbalances of power. A collaborative or participatory practice doesn't preclude the possibility of abuses of power or the replication of neoliberal values. Similarly, 'subversive' graffiti art may reproduce sexist or racist mores, readily reproducing the mainstream orthodoxies on which real inequalities are predicated.

Clichés of resistance that come from simply reproducing the orthodoxies within a particular art tradition end up reproducing the binary model of powerful–powerless. Inherent in the cliché is the idea that we are powerless and so we use the only tactics available to us. The powerful have one set of strategies; the powerless a different set of tactics.[3] This demarcation sets limits on the type of art imagined as disruptive, dissenting, and because the binary model fails to tackle ourselves as sites of both power and potential resistance, instead imagining that power always lies elsewhere, it fails to address power as we perform it.

The second reason I offer few examples of 'good' or 'political' or 'disruptive' art practices is because I refuse to fulfil that need that often surfaces in the face of critique, where solutions are required in response to the critique or 'crisis' presented. Instead, I am mindful of Ivan Illich's admonition against learned passivity, where schooling teaches us to be passive, where the master knows best and we learn to receive passively solutions from an authority. Here, I present the critique and the challenge inherent in that critique. I am grateful to all those authors who do present books of interesting resistive or disruptive art, including Grant Kester, Gregory Sholette and James Putnam,[4] because without these books I would have no access to most of the practices they cite, being the types of practice that are not widely disseminated, but this book does not perform that type of art-historical role. Instead I will argue for empowering all practitioners to make overt judgements about art based on endogenous values and to understand that we are working as an institutionalised discipline, to be honest about that fact, and to push for a disciplinary excellence, not in neoliberal terms as is the current tendency by default, but, instead, in terms of nuance and a complexity that inherently undermines orthodoxy.

The chapters break down as follows:

Chapter 1 describes how the artworld operates within the values and structures of neoliberalism and argues that this is a recent innovation. The part of the artworld that I focus on in this chapter is the monied end of the spectrum, including both the commercial gallery and auction house system and the state-sponsored international biennial exhibition system. I draw on the contributions of historians of economics and sociologists, in addition to theorists more often cited within the artworld, in order to draw out further ramifications of markets on intellectual and artistic endeavour. Like others in the artworld I am concerned by systems that reproduce inequality and that limit individual agency and freedom, as well as diversity, and I relate the story of neoliberalism not only to demonstrate how neoliberalism in fact maintains those hierarchies and exclusions despite avowing the opposite, but in order to explain the importance of doing things differently in this moment in time.

Chapter 2 recites long-established stories from the world of analytic philosophy concerning the question 'What is art?'. I bring in these theories not just because I am a fan of philosophy, which is true, but because the tradition has created a number of insights about art, art practice and the artworld that are exceptionally valuable in considering art and its role in society (the overall object of this book). While the contemporary artworld is relatively well informed about the continental philosophical tradition (for example, Karl Marx, Michel Foucault, Alain Badiou, Jacques Rancière, Slavoj Žižek), the philosophy described in Chapter 2 comes from another tradition, the analytic or Anglo-American philosophical tradition, which is relatively unknown. Yet, ironically, one debate within this tradition – on the Institutional definition of art – most accurately reflects the mechanisms and practices of the artworld.

The Institutional definition of art uniquely describes certain truths operating at the heart of the artworld. In short, the Institutional definition of art has it that the very purpose of the artworld is to define art – that is, to police its boundaries and to value its constituents. While sociological theories such as Pierre Bourdieu's about art, culture, class distinction and cultural capital have arguably, made a similar case, philosophical reasoning in the analytic tradition is useful as its inherent level of abstraction removes the specificities of period and geography.[5] The Institutional definition of art offers judgements about art beyond those of Bourdieu's. By this I do not wish to imply some kind of universality for the theory (as philosophers might), but to argue for using philosophical abstraction to help define our situation. Art is necessarily defined by a group of people called the artworld and this implies certain things about how we, as practitioners, operate and value what we do. The usefulness of the Institutional definition of art to the thesis of this book lies in its understanding of ourselves as constitutive and necessarily so. The Institutional definition of art, I would argue, reminds us that we are active in the process of defining art, not just in making art. Ever since we as artists gave up our role in defining art, preferring to imagine that anything goes within the artworld and that there are no boundaries, we have increasingly found our practice defined and valued by either the market (valued for its price as commodity) or the state (valued for its usefulness). The Institutional definition of art reminds us that we, collectively, define art and therefore we define its value.

Chapter 3 reiterates the theories of power that were taught at art school in the late 1980s. Today, art students and student curators are generally not introduced to Antonio Gramsci or the Frankfurt School, let alone to Marx, which is why I go over some of this ground here, admittedly without the nuances and subtleties. Most contemporary practitioners are not consciously aware of a history of Marxist ideas and yet certain assumptions prevail within 'ethical' or 'political' contemporary practices that stem from the strong Marxist tradition at the heart of many Western avant-garde art practices. The aim of Chapter 3 is to expose the hidden assumptions within contemporary activist art practices that stem from a largely unknown or unacknowledged theoretical legacy. A type of Marxist tradition that imagines power as located in a specific class and in specific institutions is described in Chapter 3 as a binary model of power in which one class, the ruling class with all its institutions, has all the power, while the rest are oppressed. On this model we, the avant-garde, speak on behalf of, or fight with, the oppressed against the injustices enacted by the ruling class. With few exceptions, this is the model of contemporary activism and contemporary activist art practice. Most of those engaged in the artworld who are interested in power and injustice, ethics or politics, despite citing Foucault for decades, operate as if power is located in a seemingly homogenous elite, where power is always outside of ourselves, oppressing us from the top, as if we have no volition, no agency in its operations and not as if we are ourselves constitutive of power generally or artworld mechanisms specifically. Or we imagine we are powerful and that only we can help those who are powerless or illustrate their plight. The reiteration within the contemporary artworld of binary models of power that sustained the politics and art of the 1960s and 1970s, and were also prevalent in the 1980s in the politics around Margaret Thatcher, has meant the endless re-staging of once effective and once interesting art events and the reproduction of tropes, now worn threadbare, familiar from the Conceptual Art movement. Collectively, not only are we mostly reproducing clichés in mediocre art, but politically we are failing to address power as it actually operates. Although Foucault and Rancière are referenced, the artworld operates as if the most blunt binary us–them model of power exists, ignoring our agency and, because of this, individual artists and artworld structures end up operating exactly as Foucault describes: as full and willing nodes within the mechanisms of neoliberal power.

Chapter 4 is similar to Chapter 3 in that it describes another set of assumptions, this time about what is good or bad, acceptable or unacceptable in contemporary art practice, which also stems from a strand within twentieth-century art-historical debate that is largely unacknowledged or unknown by many contemporary artists and curators. The debate is summarised in Chapter 4 as Clement Greenberg versus Allan Kaprow, though many others were also central, including those contributions to problematise the dichotomy. As in Chapter 3, the nuance and subtlety of the various positions within this debate is forfeited here – what is important to me is not so much the historiography of the debate, what was said at the time and by whom, as the consequent orthodoxies that have developed. The Frankfurt School and Gramsci might not be familiar to many art students today, so also many have heard of neither Greenberg nor Kaprow, yet their understanding of the role of art is likely to be informed by the intractable artworld dichotomy they embody, 'art' versus 'life' or aesthetics versus ethics. Chapter 4 re-examines the Greenberg–Kaprow debate in order to collapse that binary. The collapsing of binaries was a postmodern imperative and, it could be argued, has been an unthinking orthodoxy since the 1990s. As postmodern critique of the time exposed, binaries were a quotidian mechanism of the status quo maintaining, for example, gender hierarchies as well as normative pressures. However, it is not with this imperative in mind that I re-examine the binary and the assumptions created by the 'art' versus 'life' dichotomy, but to find a generative way forward: it is clear to me that the artworld operates in the shadow of this dichotomy to the detriment of both art practice and of the role of art in wider society. By collapsing the binary, re-examining its assumptions with the ideas explored in the previous chapter in mind, we may open up the possibility of a multiplicity of approaches that can be understood as having radical political or social agency and avoid reducing the importance of art in society to types of 'authentic' practice. I hope to be able to articulate a way of describing and legitimating interesting and important art that does more than simply replicate activist stereotypes and leftist clichés derived from historical circumstances and the once-potent practices that came out of them. Assumptions about art practice have been built on a framework that invests specific types of practice with an inherent radical potency while denying the possibility of radicalism to other types of practice. Inadvertently this has led to a situation where purportedly political art actually replicates neoliberal mechanisms of power and conversely where, in some cases, artwork that actually challenges dominant discourse and structures is trivialised, marginalised or overlooked by the majority of the artworld.

Chapter 5 argues for understanding art practice as a discipline akin to any other type of knowledge-forming discipline. In the face of a crisis of definition, art has been elided with activism and education and has come to be valued on those terms instead of its own. Inadvertently this has led to the replication of neoliberal mechanisms and values by the artworld, including by those who seek to challenge hierarchy, inequality and the excesses of capitalism. Whether practitioners acknowledge it or not, the artworld actually operates as an institutional discipline, in line with the Institutional definition of art; art is made within discipline-specific methodologies and with reference to discipline-specific knowledge sets, which are policed by the artworld. By understanding art practice as a knowledge-forming discipline we are better able to value what we do in endogenous terms and to judge for ourselves what is good, instead of leaving those judgements to the market or measuring ourselves within neoliberal values.

Chapter 6 concludes the book with a summary of the arguments presented in order to celebrate what is unique, and uniquely important, about art. This chapter argues that art does specific things in a society that values diversity, individual freedom and agency. In fact, art is the embodiment of a Foucauldian sense of power – both in its resistive potential and its replication of techniques of power. As resistance, art may be the embodiment of individual agency, the creation of new, nuanced, more complex stories and the potential enactment of these stories in public, constitutive of the public realm. Hannah Arendt's understanding of agency, enacted in public, I will argue is at the heart of the disruptive potential of art in society. I emphasise here the imperative of acting differently, enacting a different story and one that is not merely contrary or defined by existing power relations, in order to disrupt the dominant neoliberal grid that we happily reproduce, or indeed any dominant discourse that resists overt challenge. The power of art is in recognising the operation of power within us, which is expressed in our agency, outwardly, as stories told.

All art practices can be understood as inherently political, in that all art constitutes the social realm and any type of art practice may either support structures of power and hierarchy or otherwise. Because I am interested in disrupting systems of power that normalise inequality and orthodoxy, the art practice I am advocating here is to be understood as political in a radical sense. What is orthodox shifts over time: only those art practices that produce nuanced, complex stories that undermine or subvert today's orthodoxy are politically or socially radical and, importantly, any instances of true radicalism are unlikely to conform to artworld orthodoxies perpetuated as self-evident.

Part I
Setting the Scene

Part I contains two chapters that define this book's area of concern. The first describes the context of art practice today, namely neoliberalism; the second addresses theories of art in order to understand how the artworld actually operates as distinct from how we like to imagine it operates. The reason for spending nearly one-third of the book defining terms is because an understanding of the complexities within, and the interaction between, art and its context is fundamental to the arguments in the rest of this book. Often in books that are critical of the interaction between neoliberalism and the contemporary artworld, we find that authors spend little time defining what they mean by art and artists, and no time defining neoliberalism. I find this interesting. Clearly, for many in the artworld, the definition of art is still not to be taken for granted. It is not just the general public who find they need an explanation for its complexity and seeming arbitrariness but, ever-conscious of its boundaries, the artworld itself needs to justify what counts and what doesn't. Artists are uncomfortable in our role as police and we pretend that we allow anything to be art and anyone to be an artist, but in reality this is far from the case. By contrast, when it comes to understanding neoliberalism we either assume a common understanding of the term or that the term is simply a modish synonym for global capitalism (and then assume there's a common understanding of that). The arguments presented in this book place art in its social context in order to explore how art practice has become a mechanism of neoliberalism and, more importantly, how practitioners may do things differently.

CHAPTER 1
Neoliberalism and the Artworld

Summary

This chapter describes the economic and political structures of neoliberalism, namely privatisation, trade liberalisation and deregulation, and demonstrates how contemporary artworld structures now mimic and replicate them. This is in order to demonstrate that not only are these changes (which feel normal in the present) recent innovations but that they are pernicious. Despite the fact that many in the artworld claim a leftist politics, and some are even politically motivated to critique neoliberalism and undermine its structures, most in the artworld most of the time are actually replicating neoliberal structures and embodying and perpetuating its values. In this chapter, the artworld is described partially: only the well-financed end of the artworld spectrum features. Yet neoliberal values permeate all areas of the contemporary artworld, regardless of its financing or position within artworld hierarchy. Increased privatisation in the artworld can be seen in three interrelated areas: (1) the new dominance of the art market and the growing role played by auction houses; (2) the artworld's embrace of a funding structure that requires private money in order to receive public funding; (3) the rise of the knowledge economy. The proliferation of art biennials, large curated state-sponsored extravaganzas, is described as an instance of states parading their compliance with the neoliberal imperative to trade liberalisation (trade liberalisation is later discussed as the second aspect of neoliberalism, the first being privatisation). The discussion about deregulation (the third aspect of neoliberalism) describes an artworld that has always been a paragon of that important article of neoliberalism, namely self-regulation. I argue that, for this reason, as well as the structural changes brought about by recent changes in line with neoliberal ideology, the contemporary artworld is now exemplary of neoliberalism. We replicate its structures and its values. As this ultimately undermines any prospect for a radical or disruptive art, I describe the mechanisms and values as fully as the limited space here allows. Replicating the dominant economic and social model may not matter to some, particularly those who are to the right of politics or those 'doing well' under this system, but my argument is that, ultimately, neoliberalism equates to hierarchy and systemic exclusion, mediocrity, private monopolism and monoculturalism cloaked in values of freedom and a distorted idea of individual responsibility. It is no coincidence that the financial sector now plays a highly visible and originative role in the contemporary artworld.

◆ ◆ ◆ ◆

Neoliberalism

I will put my cards on the table: I am no economist but in my later teens I read Marx, or attempted to read him from the point of view of the Socialist International, which I had joined. During my time at art college (1987–90) a year or two later I engaged with Marxist critique. Walter Benjamin, Theodor Adorno, Louis Althusser and Antonio Gramsci were the mainstays of art education at that time. During the late 1980s, class critique was being nuanced by feminist and postcolonial critique, so these too formed part of my reading. As an art student I was expected to be conversant in the problems of the culture–power nexus. In fact, the ideological underpinnings of my art-college education contained an overt fundamental commitment to various freedoms, particularly freedom of speech, in addition to a strategic awareness of the mechanisms of power that deny the possibility of freedom. The implicit understanding was that if you believed in freedom for all equally, you more or less shared these same tools of critique: Marxist, feminist, postcolonial. It came as a big shock to me 20 years later to hear that neoliberalism draws on the same values of freedom and even equality, but from a decidedly pro-market perspective. I decided to investigate that economic, political and social ideology, despite the fact that its views come from a diametrically opposed tradition, in case it had a point. What I found is that neoliberal values permeate not just wider society but the contemporary artworld, including both the market-orientated and the politically engaged parts of the artworld, to the detriment of both freedom and equality.

Neoliberalism has had a profound effect on the artworld: on its structures, its institutions and the art market. There have also been changes in artworld discourse that could be understood as the internalisation of neoliberal values. These are described in later chapters. Here I want to concentrate on how three economic-political mechanisms of neoliberalism are played out in the artworld, namely privatisation, trade liberalisation and deregulation, with a major focus on privatisation. Critiques of the increasing market-orientation of the artworld and the increasing market-orientation of art practice have been around for decades. The amusing article 'The Rise of Andy Warhol', originally written in 1982 by Robert Hughes for *The New York Review of Books*, is a case in point.[1] What I am doing here, however, is different. I am making a connection between neoliberal values and ideology and the contemporary artworld: not only a point about greed, markets and the mediocre banal product of these markets. This features here as well, but I wish specifically to demonstrate that neoliberal mechanisms and values have been internalised by the artworld and that this is a systemic change across all types of art practice, which is creating further changes.

David Harvey's *A Brief History of Neoliberalism* charts the beginning of neoliberalism to the macro-economic innovation of monetarism of Milton Friedman in the 1960s.[2] Its rising appeal from the mid-1970s gained a sure footing in the 1980s in global economic and political structures through the policies of Margaret Thatcher in the UK and Ronald Reagan in the US. These were implemented worldwide through the World Trade Organisation (WTO) and International Monetary Fund (IMF), as described by Joseph Stiglitz, economist to the Clinton administration.[3] Though a global phenomenon, neoliberalism has a particular flavour in the UK and US, where the state itself has become 'hyperliberal', meaning that the state has been transformed to one in which 'the pattern of social power ... has realised the ascendancy of the perceived interests of the social forces of capital, particularly those groups, including financiers, seeking to expand their involvement in the world economy'.[4] In other words, wider society – its structures and discourse – reflects and reinforces the values and priorities of the financial sector. This is particularly the case in London. This chapter will describe how the artworld, as part of that wider society, has come to reflect and reinforce the values and priorities of the financial sector and the problem of this for the values of equality and difference generally, and for art specifically.

Economically, neoliberalism rests on privatisation, trade liberalisation and deregulation. Ideologically, the concept equates to a distrust of the state as provider of social goods such as health, education and the arts. Neoliberal ideology also places an emphasis on individuals rather than systems, imagining individuals as rational beings within rational systems where choices can be made. There tends to be a generalised distrust of authorities: authorities are equated with the state and regulation.

It is important to note that neoliberalism is not the same as capitalism. Briefly, neoliberalism is a set of innovations to structures that maintain a capitalist model of ownership and accumulation. Many artworld practitioners wary of capitalist excesses such as extreme inequality or environmental degradation nevertheless maintain neoliberal values and assumptions. Many artworks shown in museums and at biennial exhibitions explore anti-capitalist themes, denouncing its various exploitations; yet many of these same artists also maintain aspects of neoliberal ideology as if it is natural common sense and non-ideological. In general, the artworld supports the idea of market meritocracy, measures 'impact' and believes that the value of art lies in its social or economic impact. All these can be described as internalised neoliberal values and are new developments within artworld thinking and values. They have only come to seem axiomatic since the mid-1990s (in London).[5]

As I argue that the contemporary artworld replicates the core mechanisms within neoliberalism, it is important to be clear about what these mechanisms are. The investigation around privatisation will be broken into three parts: (1) the 'mixed economy', (2) the rise of the art market, and (3) the knowledge economy.

Privatisation and the 'mixed economy'

Privatisation is the mechanism whereby what was once owned by the public and managed on our behalf by the state is sold to private owners. Those public goods came about historically through the rise of the nation state and then, with the nineteenth century, through utilitarianism (the greatest good for the greatest number). Where parishes previously provided local, and therefore piecemeal, goods and services, public goods became standardised and universal. Infrastructure such as roads and sewers and communications such as the postal service and telephone network were public goods, owned and managed by the state; so too were trains and railways stations; aeroplanes and airports; plus telephone exchanges, lines and the telephones themselves. All the services required to keep a nation healthy and safe – such as water, waste and sanitation, prisons, law enforcement and the armed forces, plus a health and dentistry service – were at different points managed by the state on our behalf. Also, the goods that help create a better society for more people were also provided by the state, including education, welfare, the arts, parks and wildernesses. Not everything listed here is now privately owned, but there are privatised examples in every category. The very mechanism for buying and selling these things in the UK, the London Stock Exchange, was itself privatised in 1986 as part of the deregulation of the markets, known in financial circles as the 'big bang'. (The use of nature- or science-based metaphors for the financial sector and markets is a hallmark of neoliberalism, helping to make these systems and the ideological values that underwrite them seem timeless, rational or natural.)

The logic driving privatisation is that goods and services are expensive to run and become needlessly expensive or inefficient when they are run by the state. This is partly because efficiency and value for money are not top of a state's priorities. There is also an in-built conflict of interest: the state (or those who act on the public's behalf) is both the employer and the consumer of services so a fundamental conflict is said to arise in priorities. Does the state, for example, choose to pay its workers well, offer them long contracts and a generous retirement pension, which are choices predominantly in the interests of the workers, or does it try to keep costs low and cut back on employee pay and benefits so that the public pays less for its goods and services? The job of the state could be said to do both – to protect its workforce from exploitation in the interest of social stability and to protect the population against unnecessary and bad services and from unaffordable prices for public goods. This may be said to be a good or defensible reason for privatisation, because privatising public goods separates the state as consumer from the state as producer. However, there are mechanisms other than privatisation, and for which argument has been made, that could solve the problem of conflict of interest.

Instead, arguments for privatisation hinge on ideas such as those inherent in the maxim that 'competition drives innovation'. Not only are private companies said to be more efficient, which drives down costs for consumers, they are more likely to innovate new products and better services as they try to find new niches in the market or increase their market share. The state, on the other hand, because it has a captive market, does not need to provide its goods and services any differently at any point, and so it will settle on the lowest, meanest, least imaginative provision, as the Soviet Union under Stalin seemed to prove. So the argument goes, but these reasons for privatisation can be seen as ideological when looking at the evidence across the spectrum, both globally and historically. Sometimes state provision is mean, inefficient and unimaginative, and sometimes private companies provide mean, inefficient and unimaginative goods and services. Some of these goods, such as telephones and communications services, were indeed improved with privatisation in the early 1980s, although it is also true that when the imperative for universal provision was lifted, the new benefits within the telecoms industry were concentrated in London, not spread across the UK as a whole, as the patchy broadband service demonstrates. The tendency when viewing the situation from this perspective will be to downplay innovation that takes place in the public sector. Support or condemnation tends to be split on right–left political lines, and although privatisation is associated with Conservative or right-wing governments, it is a process that was accelerated by the leftist governments in the 1990s and 2000s in the UK and US, those of Tony Blair and Bill Clinton respectively. The reasons for its implementation are based on assumptions about state and market models that are neoliberal *and* ideological, given that the evidence substantiating these assumptions is mixed.

In the case of arts funding, it was New Labour that introduced the compulsion for arts organisations to seek private money – be it sponsorship, 'self-generated income' or donation – *in order* to receive public money. This type of funding model, known euphemistically as a 'mixed economy' model, became 'best practice' across the arts, culture, museums and heritage sector, and the ideal promulgated by the artworld for the rest of the sector, which remained ambivalent.[6] It is notable that prior to the wholesale acceptance of the New Labour funding model, the artworld shared a general scepticism around funding of the arts. 'He who pays the piper plays the tune' was the arts' maxim and only an arm's length disinterest was acceptable in Britain prior to the New Labour model. When the Arts Council of Great Britain was formed in 1946, there had been a distance between the arts and government funding arrangements and this distance had been respected by governments of all hues until 1997 when the rationale for arts funding was dramatically altered. For the first time, funding became linked not to an artworld elite's self-defined notion of excellence, but instead to increasing the range and type of audience for the arts (known as 'access') and, to a lesser extent, to those activities that provide social goods such as 'community cohesion'. The full range of the debate around a new perceived dichotomy – access and excellence – can be seen in *Art For All? Their Policies and Our Culture* (2000).[7] What the debate demonstrates is the neoliberal sleight of hand around democratic values of freedom and equality, which will be described further in a later section. The new dichotomy became politicised so that excellence is understood as potentially elitist, old-fashioned and right wing, whereas 'access' is new, inclusive, democratic and/or left wing. Although the argument at the time was for the access agenda to be balanced by the excellence agenda, when a tension was perceived it was access that must prevail because access had a prescribed funding target.

As such, the 'mixed economy' model – with its pressure to stage exhibitions with mass popular appeal that ensure both corporate sponsorship and ticket sales as self-generated income – can be shown to have determined the types of exhibitions staged. Tate Modern is a high-profile and dramatic case in point. In 2001 the Director, Lars Nittve, stated an ambition for Tate Modern that it would 'widen our cultural perspective, from a Western concept of internationalism – in the case of modern museums often synonymous, embarrassingly enough, with NATO alliance – to one which is truly worldwide'.[8] To do so, Tate Modern initiated a variety of bold, innovative exhibitions such as 'Century City' (2001).[9] By 2006, it was clear that the trend was in the opposite direction, towards strategies for 'access' over Tate Modern's self-defined ideas of excellence (where access was defined through the New Labour directive to 'reflect success in self-generated income, [and] sponsorship' as well as increased audience numbers).[10] The temporary exhibitions programme, which in the beginning had been innovative for the range and breadth of artists from across the globe, congealed around white males from (embarrassingly enough) NATO countries. The number of women artists shown had fallen and the range of countries from which artists hailed decreased.

An assumption was made that audiences would more likely flock to exhibitions of approximately ten named artists – all dead white men (with the exception of Frida Kahlo) – including Matisse, Picasso, Warhol, Monet and Dalí, and that audiences in great numbers were less likely to attend more innovative exhibition programmes. Looking carefully at the statistics provided by Tate Modern, there is little evidence to substantiate this assumption. Instead, there is a correlation between corporate-sponsored exhibitions, larger marketing budgets and total audience figures, implying that it is not necessarily audiences who have conservative tastes in art, but corporate sponsors and museums programmers in fear of losing public subsidy.[11]

Privatisation and the rise of the art market

Over the mid-1990s and 2000s a growing accommodation and acceptance of privatisation in the form of an increasing dominance of the art market occurred within the artworld. There came to be a reliance on the market as the sole arbiter of artistic value, even within public art institutions that had previously retained some independence from the market, operating with their own criteria for 'good' or museum-quality art. Although museum preferences often overlapped with the preferences of the art market, this was not always the case. Publicly funded galleries and museums worked with criteria derived mostly from the writing of art historians and critics, and while many critically acclaimed or historically important artists were part of the commercial system, not everyone was. For example, artists such as Sonia Boyce (the last artist without commercial representation to be shown at Tate Modern) had a different pathway to being considered a museum-quality artist. She was part of a generation shown in 'alternative' and publicly funded galleries, who had no presence within the market system.

Up until the 2000s there had been a clear alternative to the commercial galleries. These alternative galleries, wholly public funded, showed a different set of artists from the commercial galleries and often a different type of art. Similarly, a generation before that, the commercial centre for art in London, Cork Street, sold a different kind of art from the avant-garde practices exhibited down the road at the Institute of Contemporary Art (ICA). Founded in 1947 and supported by the Arts Council since 1968, the ICA was an important site for those avant-garde practices that were understood as inherently anti-commercial because of their politics or non-commercial because they were experimental. In other words, throughout the twentieth century until the late 1990s, it was either the state that picked up the small bill for experimental, critical or avant-garde practices or the artworld created its own structures through squats and cheap studios, shops and warehouse spaces, plus an amount of direct patronage.[12]

Historically, there has always been a connection between the avant-garde and the market, but structural and conceptual changes that happened in the new millennium now afford no alternative to the market and market ideology. It is this that is new and, notably, this lack of alternative is an ambition of neoliberalism. Francis Fukuyama's famous 1989 essay 'The End of History' parades this ambition.[13] Over the 2000s, for the first time since the 'historical avant-garde' as Peter Bürger calls it,[14] the avant-garde was no longer structurally or conceptually alternative to anything, being almost entirely located within the overtly commercial art fairs and their 'education' wings or in the covertly commercial, state economic- and investment-growth orientated biennials. Since the 2000s only those art initiatives located in institutions or with institutional backing were considered 'legitimate' even by activist and politically radical artists. If, for example, ArtsAdmin, Artangel or Live Art Development Agency didn't back it, then there was no way to know if an artwork (or even a piece of art activism) was good. All artistic practices without institutional support became invisible and even radical activist artists feel this as failure rather than the success that previous generations bolstered by Romantic myths of genius could rationalise. Gregory Sholette's *Dark Matter*, which uses a Marxist analysis of surplus labour to describe the US artworld, demonstrates the cold comfort within contemporary artworld discourse of failure in neoliberal terms.[15]

Perhaps it is also true that the avant-garde of each generation since the 'historical avant-garde' of the 1920s and 1930s is bound to disappoint. One might deduce this from Bürger's critique of the avant-garde of his time – that is, the avant-garde of 1974. Ironically, for many contemporary artists and historians revelling in a nostalgia for past artistic potency, 1974 seems a high point.

My argument is that at the same time as the contemporary artworld began to share the structures of neoliberalism, the values within the artworld became overtly commercial and indistinguishable from those of the commercial sector. Market discourse became the only way to legitimate 'good' or museum quality and this is anomalous within the history of Modernism. The Arts Council, perhaps being self-conscious of this, published *Market Matters* in 2004 in which Louisa Buck wrote that 'there has always been some relationship between public sector art institutions and the art market'.[16] This is true. The distance between the avant-garde and the market has been overstated historically, usually for political reasons, but it is also true that there is now an historically unprecedented fusion of the public sector with the commercial market, a phenomenon that has happened in London only since the 2000s, concurrent with the dominance of neoliberal values in both the artworld and wider society. The Arts Council simply exemplified this in publishing *Market Matters* and in subsequent publications.[17] Since 2000, London has become a primary centre for the global art market. Tate Modern opened in 2000, followed by a sharp increase in commercial galleries opening in its shadow; Frieze Art Fair began in 2003 followed by imitators such as Zoo Art Fair (2004–9). Also at this time there was a marked change in the importance of the tertiary market – the auction houses – for the artworld. Suddenly, what happened on the tertiary market mattered. A few artists have bypassed the commercial gallery system (the primary market) entirely in favour of the greater financial rewards and apparent freedoms of the auction houses, a strategy initiated by Damien Hirst's *Beautiful Inside My Head Forever* sale at Sotheby's in London in 2008.

For some, like the market anthropologist Olav Velthuis, this is a good development. Pro-market Velthuis believes the whole commercial gallery system should be as transparent as the auction houses by allowing the market to establish prices instead of the commercial galleries.[18] He goes on to observe that the primary market, meaning the commercial gallery system, has a further impact: in the absence of any other type of legitimating value for art practice, the primary market establishes not only 'economic and artistic values' but 'historical standing' as well because of the relationship between primary and secondary markets.[19]

The reality of the primary art market contrasts with a neoliberal article of faith: that the market is meritocratic and democratic, operating within the simple rules of supply and demand so that an artist's value is high because demand is high but supply is limited. This is propounded by art-market advocates such as the former journalist and Art Basel Co-Director, Marc Spiegler, and the influential monthly publication *The Art Newspaper*, which claim that the art market operates as any market is supposed to: in reality the mechanisms of the art market are distorted. It is not an open market but a closed, elite system subject to a level of insider trading and price-fixing, which is illegal in any other arena. Critical of the practices of commercial galleries, Velthuis writes that:

> The fact that supply and demand do not interact directly to set prices on the primary market is considered [by the commercial galleries] to be a vice, but a virtue at the same time: it enables a sense of structure to the market, and keeps the uncertainty that prevails about the value of art under control.[20]

Velthuis' observations about the primary market's control over art's wider value are damning. Citing another pro-market anthropologist, Stuart Plattner, Velthuis writes that 'the bankruptcy of art criticism and evaluative art theory ... means that value is mysterious, socially constructed, and impossible to predict' in a way that has no equivalent in other markets.[21] Commercial galleries fix prices for art, claiming that this insulates artists against the pressures created by the vagaries of an open market. An artist's talent might not withstand either big hikes or great drops in price, so the primary market ensures a steady, lifetime increase in price for the artist.

Operating slightly differently is the market for the biennials. Sociologist Pascal Gielen describes the normative mechanisms at play in the biennial market, which may be more innovative compared with the art of the auction houses but the biennial market is also less than open.[22] It operates as a highly concentrated, organised, closed system. Biennial exhibitions such as the Venice Biennale, are large extravaganzas which, as they are state-sponsored, have different funding arrangements from the commercial sector. Nevertheless, biennials need to attract corporate sponsorship, and the artists involved are often also part of the commercial gallery system. Artists' income is less from selling objects and ideas than from commissions that may be either temporary or permanent. In *The Murmuring of the Artistic Multitude: Global Art, Memory and Post-Fordism*, Gielen quotes from various interviews he has conducted with curators and gallerists. I reproduce a few of them here as they neatly illustrate the point about the artworld as a closed system:

> When you know something about the art context, you can start easily. You have to keep an eye on the best galleries, museum and the selection of some curators to make a somewhat acceptable selection. In fact, to do so, you do not have to know anything about art.
>
> *Richard Foncke, 2001*[23]

> In the art world a lot depends, too, on who you are and what you've already done. Of course, they phone their colleagues to ask who you are ...
>
> *Barbara Vanderlinden, 2001*[24]

> I have a very good relationship with Anton Herbert, who is also on my advisory board. But I also have good contacts with Daled and Goeminne [collectors]. It's my job to keep myself informed about developments in the art world, after all.
>
> *Jan Debbaut, 2001*[25]

> Curator x, he is a case of pure networking. He once stole the list of addresses from Documenta. Whether this is gossip or not ... it is characteristic of him. He knows nothing about art. He cannot see.
>
> *Jan Hoet, 2000*[26]

Gielen's work describes how the biennial and museum part of the artworld operates as a closed, concentrated and organised market. The deleterious effects of this type of market operation, specifically on diversity and creativity, are described by the French economist Jean Gadrey and market sociologist Michel Callon.

Gadrey is sympathetic to markets but with 'precautionary principles' in order to preserve diversity and innovation. He describes how the market will tend to reproduce endless variations on the 'same basic matrices or products'.[27] In order to guarantee their markets, they suppress any innovation that has a different starting point. The art that tops the league tables as favoured by the auction houses demonstrates his point. With but little amendment, it can all be described as an endless variation on the same basic matrix: a type of pop art with representational elements, often referencing pop culture or brands, combined with an advertising-campaign-type of 'twist'. In the twentieth century, this might only describe art from the West, but in a globalised art market, it is an equally apt description for the most highly priced work of artists from emerging economies, such as Zhang Xiaogang or Yue Minjun: endless monocultural variations in the guise of shared values. Gadrey writes:

> Markets [have an] inability to create, on a commercial basis, all the intellectual, cultural and social conditions for economic and social development of sufficient quality and variety to be sustainable. Markets are powerful and flexible and can offer freedom in the short term, however, they are reductive, since they need to stabilise the identity of their objects, of their agents and of the framework within which their reckonings take place.[28]

For Gadrey, it is a balance and variety of systems that is required for a diversity of innovation. Any monopolistic authority – be it the market, the state or academia – will succeed in reducing plurality or diversity.[29] Prior to the neoliberal mechanisms of the 'mixed economy' model, there had been some plurality in the London artworld, as publicly funded art was different from market-supported art. In fact, public galleries supported those artists who even today are least represented by the art market, namely women and artists with non-NATO backgrounds and from outside the economic centres of power. At auction, the market values art by men as, on average, ten times more valuable than comparable women artists';[30] there is significant under-representation of black artists by London commercial galleries, with Victoria Miro Gallery being one of the few exceptions. At the 2007 conference 'The Rise of the London Art Market', held at Tate Britain, market bias was openly discussed. Louisa Buck mentioned that the commercial gallery system is far from representative of all art practices and avoids what she termed 'less market-friendly artists'. Matthew Slotover of *Frieze* (the art magazine and the art fair) concurred, adding that since the early 1990s commercial galleries have become increasingly risk-averse despite a booming market, speculating that this was because of the weight of greater financial pressure.

Within the discourse of neoliberalism, there is a supposed neutrality to the operation of the markets. They are supposed to reward what is best or most promising without prejudice or favour. This is why they are supposed to be meritocratic. The innovative will find a niche even in a market with huge sharks or big fish, whichever is the preferred piscine metaphor. Economists Jonathan Nitzan and Shimshon Bichler have shown the opposite: a free unregulated market will tend to monopoly where big fish eat all the viable little fish.[31] The natural metaphor that market apologists tend to favour is not applicable: in nature, diversity forms the basis of a dynamic equilibrium – there is a balance. In markets, the tendency is towards corporate monopoly and monoculture.

Michel Callon, a market sociologist, is interested in market relationships to scientific research. His work has informative parallels for the artworld. The more organised and concentrated a market, the less diverse and open it will be. He writes, 'It is only when certain options have been eliminated and that the range of options has been drastically reduced, that the market is finally organised.'[32] Because the market generalises in order to kill off other potential ones, and puts in place various forms of cooperation with the aim of sharing uncertainties, goods and processes tend to become standardised. Callon writes:

> The agents who manage to occupy key positions draw the boundaries of competition, eliminate competitors, select technologies and thus capture the demand. ... We cannot show more clearly that the very nature of competition is to rarefy competition.[33]

This in turn gives rise to irreversibility that reduces the range of options, such as the QWERTY keyboard, or it leads to the ubiquity of inferior products, such as Microsoft MS-DOS.[34] The art market is highly organised and self-regulating, enacting all the pitfalls Callon predicts for a concentrated market for science and technology, including a lack of true diversity. Callon writes:

> The simple decision to invest in a given technology [for technology read art practice] sets off a dynamic of learning and accumulation which rapidly leads to unequal development. The chosen technology becomes increasingly attractive and profitable, not by virtue of its intrinsic qualities, but because substantial investments have been devoted to it ... [35]

Without an artworld discourse of value that comes from within the artworld and not from the market, and without any other form of support for art other than the market, there is nothing to check market excesses, monoculturalism and mediocrity.

Since the 2000s, markets have been described and promoted as dynamic and innovative whereas the state is perceived to be an instrumentalising organ. Critics of the New Labour government's policies for the arts, such as Andrew Brighton and Munira Mirza, argued against New Labour's instrumentalisation of the arts to ameliorate social ills.[36] These criticisms may have been largely correct, if rhetorically exaggerated, but their arguments against state intervention in the arts also furthered the impression that any state involvement in the arts is bad for innovation and that the alternative, therefore, which is the market, must be good or at least preferable. These assumptions are instances of neoliberal ideology. In a piece of gross *reductio ad absurdum*, because the state is interfering in artistic freedoms, it is assumed the market does not.

Privatisation and the knowledge economy

The 1990s saw the advent of the knowledge economy, another aspect of neoliberalism and the privatisation of knowledge as intellectual property (IP). This aspect of privatisation, the buying and selling of IP and the vast increase in IP as a form of commodity, has deep implications for the artworld. Although knowledge has been an economic product in its own right since 1986 (through 'TRIPS', International Trade in Intellectual Property[37]), IP has become vitally important to the economies of the West since 1997. The emphasis on knowledge as property meant that the West could prevent jobs moving from the developed world to the cheaper developing world, as had occurred with manufacturing and other material-based sectors such as mining.[38] With the increased growth of the knowledge economy, there became a greater emphasis on all forms of IP – including art, patents and software, and anything that can be written down or documented such as ideas – as ripe for commodification or monetisation.

This had a real implication for artists. Since the beginning of copyright law, art, and specifically printed material including books, has been implicated in ideas of property and ownership, but traditionally this revolved around conventional art forms and specific ideas of originality.[39] By the end of the 1980s, with the eighth round of General Agreement on Tariffs and Trade (GATT) talks well under way, out of which the knowledge economy was born, it is possible to refer legally to 'dematerialised property', thus enabling the 'dematerialised' to become part of the normative, legal systems for protecting and trading property.[40] This innovation in the concept of property came about through the perceived necessity to protect computer software from what came to be perceived as theft, and the artworld also played its part in driving forward IP law. Art theorist Jaime Stapleton describes how one permutation of 1970s, politically radical art, namely 'appropriation art', was used in the case of Rogers vs. Koons (1989–92).[41] Until the advent of the knowledge economy, an artist could choose to make art using low-value materials such as refuse, or an artist could make art from concepts alone as a strategy for refusal, a strategy to avoid the process of commodification and the market. This tactic, common to Dada, Arte Povera, Fluxus, Mail Art and Conceptual Art, was no longer available once anything, even an idea, was property and therefore potentially monetisable.[42] With the rise of the knowledge economy even the idea of future sales or profits could be traded, a further level of monetisation exemplified by the 'Bowie Bond' through which David Bowie received US $55 million against future royalties from 25 albums.[43]

David Bowie's Bowie Bonds of 1997 seemingly had a precursor in Marcel Duchamp's 'bonds'. In 1924 Duchamp issued bonds (complete with a photograph by Man Ray of Duchamp as Hermes, god of gaming, with face and wings sculpted in soap suds). Duchamp's bonds were issued arguably both in order to fund his Monte Carlo gambling pursuits and as part of a Dadaist critique of the institution of art, and perhaps it goes without saying that Duchamp's bonds had no relationship with the financial markets of the time. The difference between then and now is that the immaterial, or the 'dematerialized' to use Lucy Lippard's coinage for just this type of practice of refusal, is inherently property, commodifiable and monetisable as part of larger market innovations with the knowledge economy.[44] In fact, taken together, a comparison between Bowie's bonds and Duchamp's illustrates the differences in the social-political-economic context between then and now. For the first time in history, no type of art practice stands *a priori* outside property law. In other words, a potent political strategy used since the 1920s by the avant-garde – that is, the use of ephemera and inherently valueless materials to make art that is both actually and symbolically beyond the ken of commodification – was disabled. The implications of this for politically radical artists working today are described further in Chapter 4. With the various forms of privatisation within the artworld consequent of neoliberalism – the privatisation of public funding, the privatisation of art's value with the dominance of the art market and the privatisation of knowledge – long-established 'alternatives' to capitalism and the status quo, as well as modes of dissent, no longer exist because the structures that enable them no longer exist.

Trade liberalisation and the artworld

Trade liberalisation is the dismantling of barriers to trade and production across national borders. This is contrasted with protectionism, which is when countries protect goods produced at home against foreign competition by, for example, having tariffs on foreign imports so they cost more. Without liberalisation, states might create laws that favour local products or services or they might ban foreign imports altogether. The state also might restrict exports of raw materials, so favouring local manufacturers using local versions, or they may subsidise local producers.

In terms of the artworld, it is the biennials in particular that demonstrate a country's commitment to trade liberalisation. These art events both signify and enact a country's trade liberalism by bringing together the cultural products of various nations and celebrating them equally as emblems of shared values. These shared values may include liberal, democratic ones such as freedom of speech but, primarily, art biennials demonstrate effectively that a country aims to function within the rules of neoliberalism: liberalisation, privatisation and deregulation. Once occurring only in Western cultural centres, there has been an explosion in the amount and variety of biennial hosts beginning with the rise of the knowledge economy and accelerating with the new millennium. The first biennial state-sponsored extravaganza was in Venice in 1895, followed by the Whitney Museum, New York, in 1932 and Documenta at Kassel in 1955. Biennials now occur in Asia (the first one in Gwangju in 1995, Taipei in 1998, Shanghai international since 2000 and Singapore in 2006);[45] the Middle East (Istanbul in 1987 and Sharjah in 1993);

Africa (Dakar in 1992, Johannesburg 1995, Marrakech 2005); Latin America (Havana 1984 and Ushuaia, Tierra del Fuego 2007) – and even this is not a comprehensive list. To date there are approximately 100 biennials globally.

Not only have neoliberal structures and ideology steered the course for an increase or deepening of markets across the globe generally, and specifically in India, Brazil, China and Russia, but it is evident that with this increased marketisation there has been an increase in the art markets within and for these countries. Where there was once no market for contemporary art within China, India, Brazil and Russia, nor was there a market for these 'regional' artists in the major Western art centres, there is now a thriving interest in the art from these countries, with Russia topping the league table for most expensive modernist woman artist, Natalya Goncharova, and China ahead in the global league tables for amounts fetched for (male) artists. In 2009, Chinese artists Zhang Xiaogang, Zeng Fanzhi and Yue Minjun came fifth, sixth and seventh in terms of turnover in euros – after Jeff Koons, Jean-Michel Basquiat, Damien Hirst and Richard Prince, in that order.[46] It is important to note that while each of these countries had their own thriving artworld and Modernisms prior to neoliberalism, they did not have developed art markets.

Trade liberalisation supports the myth of market meritocracy: that everything of value will find a niche and the highest price is paid for the best. Allowing that other global centres produce art of international museum quality demonstrates the ideal that there are no structural biases to markets and the general good of neoliberalism. Today's art market, unlike the elitist, Eurocentric markets of past generations, supposedly supports any type of art from anywhere in the world, exemplifying the myth of market meritocracy.[47] The biennials are there to prove there is a level playing field for creative greatness. Moreover, in the case of those biennials staged by the more repressive regimes, they signpost a certain tolerance on a global stage and, at an elite level, for an amount of political liberalism – the type of tolerance and 'democracy' that trade liberalisation and exposure to Western economic models is assumed to produce. Of course, Venice *Biennali* have long been established as a platform for national posturing and 'cultural diplomacy' and these newer biennials may be understood similarly, but they may also be understood specifically as an instance of the new neoliberal structures of the artworld and the general artworld acceptance of these as normal, natural, good.[48]

Deregulation and the artworld

Deregulation is the drive to self-regulation, where a sector or industry creates and polices the rules by which it operates. This is opposed to regulation by the state, which is legally binding, carries sanctions and is referred to as 'red tape' by those opposed. According to the logic of deregulation, it is in the interest of both consumers and producers to self-regulate as this streamlines business: business can operate more smoothly with minimal government laws and regulation. In general, regulation is understood as creating outside 'exogenous' stipulations or artificial obstacles, whereas self-regulation is self-determined, when an industry has its own standards of practice in order to function as a business or serve its public better. Rather than laws and regulations, it is consumers who produce the checks and balances necessary to a well-functioning industry and the wider economy. If the public does not want covertly obtained private information, for example, they will stop buying the newspapers that sell it. Shareholders will be the brakes on banking overexuberance.

Historically, government regulation was a response to the events of the 1930s' Great Depression when it became clear that one of the roles of the state was the protection of citizens against the excesses of business as usual when business is no longer serving its customers. Importantly, at that time it came to be understood widely that markets have cycles, which at their low ebb are catastrophic, particularly for the poorer sections of society. Despite this, proponents of deregulation claim that citizens need no state protection when they act as consumers because consumers can provide the necessary checks and balances, whereas states are unduly autocratic and authoritarian when they regulate free enterprise. According to this thinking, states often get it wrong and it is their interference in markets that creates the catastrophic consequences. Economists who favour this view, following Friedrich Hayek, tend to cite President George W. Bush's interference in the housing market as a case in point. It is argued that Bush's policy that every American should own their own home created, or at least fostered, the 'subprime' loans and mortgage market, which when sold on in investment packages as 'collateralised debt obligations' (CDOs) globally, created the 2008 Global Financial Crisis and the ongoing catastrophic consequences for the economy worldwide, and particularly for Europe and the US. Proponents of regulation argue that this is faulty logic, as regulations interrupt corporate excesses regardless of the conditions that created them.

The artworld has always been a form of deregulated market. No one outside the artworld determines the definition of art or determines what constitutes quality in art practice. The artworld maintains its right to police the boundary of art. Chapter 2 will describe what 'regulates' art in the London artworld, namely a diffuse operation of power through discourse and social mechanisms, and the implications of this for contemporary art practice. In Britain, there has never been real government interference in the matter of how art is defined, how the artworld polices itself or how and where it is exhibited. Perhaps cultural production in the UK has rarely been seen as so important as to require external regulation. Alternatively, it may be that because freedom is a defining concept underpinning art, any regulation of art and culture is understood as the hallmark of a repressive society. Whichever is the reason, modern British governments generally avoid interfering (despite New Labour's instrumentalisation of the arts and previous governments' regimes of censorship of sex and nudity, which must be understood as trivial when compared with the suppression enacted within authoritarian regimes).

The artworld can be seen as a paragon of deregulation at work. It is the artworld that defines art, solely determining its definition and its value. But we have also seen how neoliberal structural changes encourage both acceptance of prevailing market discourse and the narrowing of diversity across art practices. Art practice has become more or less standardised globally. This monoculturalism and inevitable mediocrity must be understood as the product of the implementation of market mechanisms for valuing art, including within the publicly funded sector, and that the authority that describes art's values, definition and worth is now placed in one location, namely the market.

It is no coincidence that with the rise in neoliberalism there was a growth in both the contemporary art market and the biennial market. Global financial structures produced an ultra-rich elite with money to squander on hyper-inflated objects. 'New markets' produced oligarchs, and market ideology legitimated their wealth and their status. Following other plutocrats from history, the new plutocrats validate their wealth and position by purchasing culture. At first the Russian oligarchs, for example, bought into established Western art values, then they created new ones through new markets in local variations: in the late 2000s, Natalya Goncharova attracted the highest prices for a woman artist at auction, overtaking Frida Kahlo's top position. Market apologists cite the Borgias and their funding of great Renaissance art, but, historically and globally, great wealth has sponsored both greatness and great mediocrity.

Conclusion

Today's contemporary art signifies innovations within capitalism, as Luc Boltanski and Ève Chiapello have described in *The New Spirit of Capitalism*.[49] Those ultra-rich who made their money in investment banking and new markets purchase contemporary avant-garde art because it embodies free, unregulated markets and capitalist innovation.

What interests me is two things. First, how the majority of the artworld – who are far from served by these recent neoliberal structural changes – have come to accept them as normal, even desirable, and how artworld values now incorporate neoliberal values. While subsequent chapters describe how neoliberal values such as measurement came to be absorbed by the artworld, including by those on the left, my emphasis here has been on structural changes, which have meant that the contemporary artworld now exemplifies neoliberalism. The recent involvement of bankers and hedge fund managers in the contemporary art market may be neither coincidence nor the simple product of the fact that contemporary art is yet another lucrative investment. Perhaps the reason that contemporary art now occupies a highly visible and central role in the financial district lies in the recent convergence of values. Once operating with distinct, separate world views and narratives, the artworld is now 'hyperliberal', to use Paul Langley's term for how the interests of the financial district are echoed and promulgated in other parts of society. The artworld is now a paragon of neoliberalism, whether or not its players understand this – and even when oppositional politics are espoused. To quote Michael Sandel, 'markets leave their mark on social norms, driving out all other values'.[50]

CHAPTER 2

We Who Police the Definition and Value of Art

Summary

By the end of the twentieth century, the idea of art no longer implied the pursuit of values such as truth and beauty, nor did it require specific materials such as paint or marble. No type of material or object lay outside of art's ever-increasing definition, including urinals and excrement, and no process was excluded either, including the planting of trees or the cutting of one's body. For a generation or two, art has apparently been made of anything and it has been made by anybody. 'Everyone is an artist' goes the cliché. Yet people working in the artworld – artists, curators, dealers, collectors, educators, writers – know this isn't strictly true and some of us live with this knowledge uncomfortably. Over the same period, a particular strand in the Anglo-American tradition of aesthetic philosophy has been dealing with the anomalies presented by the artworld and it is our loss that, in general, these ideas are not widely known. Being aware of this would help us understand and reconcile ourselves to the seeming paradoxes within contemporary art practice, which those of us on the left – who believe in inclusion as a democratic ideal and yet who participate in an artworld filled with exclusions – find difficult. This chapter brings the Institutional definition of art to an artworld audience, not only in order to explain the mechanisms operating that allow inclusions into and exclusions from the definition of art, but because it demonstrates that the very definition of art is a social process, that this policing is what we do, even when we deny it or wish it were otherwise. In understanding that the definition of art is subject to social pressures and discourse, we see that although no single person or institution has the power to define art, together and collectively we each contribute to its definition. This is an important idea in that it allows us to understand ourselves as agents, not passively receiving artworld beneficence or neglect, but as constituting it. If art now shares neoliberal values and mechanisms, it is by definition the product of our choices and not something imposed from the outside or a phenomenon over which we have no volition.

◆ ◆ ◆ ◆

Artists and the philosophy of art

The definition of art has been contested in the Western philosophical tradition since Plato. While definitions of art are generally the purview of philosophers who attempt to extract eternal verities from the morass of experience, at times artists also enter the fray. There is a line of artists, from Schiller to Wagner, Guy Debord to Barnett Newman, writing in order to redefine or reposition what they do and why they do it and whose writings then help to define art philosophically. This chapter will demonstrate why this act of writing is vital and important, not only for an understanding of art from the point of view of artists, but for its very definition as described in the Institutional definition of art, which comes from the analytic tradition of philosophy.

There is a schism in philosophy circles. There is the analytic or Anglo-American tradition and there is the continental tradition. So deep is the schism, that in British universities it can be difficult to find anyone who engages seriously with both. London-based artists, if we read any philosophy, draw on the continental tradition that covers, for example, Marx, Foucault, Badiou and Rancière. To explain why the Anglo-American tradition is overlooked by the London artworld, I might blame its heavy emphasis on Logic, but Anglo-American aesthetics seems to be ignored primarily for historical reasons, on the grounds that it maintains formalist and untenably elitist discourse. With the ascendency of Conceptual Art in the 1960s and 1970s, and artists' contempt for philosophers such as Clive Bell and Clement Greenberg, came an assumption that the Anglo-American tradition offers nothing for the artworld.[1] Artist John Latham held a party in 1967 at which people were invited to chew up a library copy of Greenberg's *Art and Culture*, returning it (masticated) in phials to the art-college library as an artwork entitled *Art and Culture*.

In this chapter I draw on the analytic tradition, specifically Ludwig Wittgenstein, Arthur Danto and George Dickie, in order to define and understand what is art. Compared with the continental tradition, analytic philosophy is abstracted and idealised: philosophical truths occur in the realm of ideas with little or no social or political relation. Analytic philosophy is not meant to be empirical, informed by or based on sensory observation, but on thinking alone. In contrast, the continental tradition considers, and even foregrounds, the social and political. This is another reason the artworld has little cognisance of the analytic tradition: since the late 1960s most in the artworld work self-consciously within their social and political context, whether that is the market, popular culture or radical politics. Danto and Dickie are both exponents of the 'Institutional definition of art', but it is Dickie who comes to a conclusion that is almost untenable within the analytic tradition: not only does he acknowledge the role of the social but he makes it central to the very definition of art. For those schooled in the continental tradition, however, Dickie doesn't go far enough: he doesn't reflect on the political implications of the theory. Namely, who constitutes the artworld, who and what are excluded, in other words, what is not art. This chapter marries the two traditions in the way that they both offer important insights for the artworld as it operates today: the analytic for its strength in analysing concepts in the abstract, using logic and thought to understand the world as it is, and the continental for its strength in locating these ideas in social reality and pursuing their political implications.

Aesthetics and the analytical philosophical tradition

The artworld favours two maxims: 'everyone is an artist' and art is 'anything defined as art'. Often attributed to Joseph Beuys in the late 1960s, these maxims were, however, promulgated throughout the Romantic period, including in Wagner's 1849 text, 'Art and Revolution'.[2] The 'anything goes' definition of art has democratic and anti-elitist implications. Creativity is not the purview of one class, nation or gender. In the analytic philosophical tradition, Wittgenstein could be said to substantiate philosophically this 'anything goes'.

Wittgenstein describes language as a set of *language-games* within which the words of a language function and receive their meaning. Meaning is created through use. A word simply means something because that is how it is used in language. This idea replaced the classical one by which meaning was understood as representation: a word represents a thing, feeling, attribute. Morris Weitz, working in the Wittgensteinian tradition, argues that art cannot be defined in the traditional sense of shared qualities or values; instead, he claims it is an 'open concept' and comparable with other open concepts like games.[3] An open concept is a set of family resemblances where one thing might be similar to a second, and a third is similar to the second but the third and the first have little in common. Things that are 'art' share this type of family resemblance.[4] In this way, an Italian Renaissance chapel painting, the 24,000-year-old *Willendorf Venus* sculpture found in Austria and John Cage's *4 minutes and 33 seconds* of silence are all instances of 'art'. This account seems to allow for the multiplicity of approaches, practices and products contained within a working definition of art. It is the philosophy for everyone-is-an-artist but it does not account for why, in reality, only some objects and practices are valued as art. Although Wittgenstein's philosophy is useful for explaining what is already considered art, it is not useful in attempting to discover why one thing is art while another isn't, particularly under those conditions when an object may not be immediately understood as art. For this, the Institutional definition of art provides a philosophical contribution, with Arthur Danto and George Dickie as the two main rivalling exponents of the theory. One emphasises the role of writing; the other the role of social processes and both versions have implications for understanding the mechanisms operating in the contemporary artworld.

Arthur Danto and the Institutional definition of art

Danto came to understand the centrality of discourse in the very perception of art when he considered his response to the philosophical shock of first encountering Andy Warhol's *Brillo Boxes* in 1964. The paradox that occurs when two sets of materially indistinguishable objects – a grocer's Brillo boxes and Warhol's *Brillo Boxes* – are exactly the same but only one is art, was resolved with the idea that it is criticism, philosophy or theory that makes one art and the other not art. Danto wrote that 'to see something as art requires something the eye cannot descry – an atmosphere of artistic theory, a knowledge of the history of art: an artworld'.[5] There is nothing in the materiality of the object that makes one art and the other not art. There is nothing in the techniques used or the aesthetic of the finished object. There is no quality that is necessary for making one thing art and another not art: no aesthetic, practice or craft. It is discourse which makes art. Danto wrote:

> What in the end makes the difference between a Brillo box and a work of art consisting of a Brillo Box is a certain theory of art ... It is the role of artistic theories, these days as always, to make the artworld, and art, possible. It would, I should think, never have occurred to the painters of Lascaux that they were producing *art* on those walls. Not unless there were neolithic aestheticians. [6]

Danto's observation is that it is philosophy, or writing about art *as art*, that is required as an *a priori* condition to *art*-making. Art requires the writing and thinking about art to exist, otherwise objects are understood, even perceived, as something else.

Examples of this can be seen throughout the twentieth and twenty-first centuries. For example, the period during the late 1960s and 1970s saw a proliferation of artist and theorist writing around Conceptual Art. Theorists and historians such as Victor Burgin, Lucy Lippard and Benjamin Buchloh defined the Conceptual Art project along with artist-theorists such as Art & Language. Meanwhile, artists such as Yoko Ono, Sol LeWitt and Adrian Piper demonstrated through their writing how well they performed within this new definition of art. Others, such as John Latham and Barbara Steveni of Artist Placement Group, challenged the boundaries of art by operating with reference to the new legitimating discourse. We can see a similar process happening more recently with theorists, curators and artists of the late 1990s and 2000s, such as Claire Bishop, Nicolas Bourriaud, Claire Doherty, Jane Rendell, Gregory Sholette, Suzanne Lacy and Grant Kester. They too ended up redefining art by articulating a new definition of art and the value of what was called ethically or socially engaged art practices; writing and defining art anew. Just as Danto describes, together they can be understood as having created a new type of politicised art practice called, among other terms, relational or dialogic. Collectively they did this by creating a body of legitimating artworld discourse, with the result that politicised art practice, and even activism, was seen in UK galleries subsequently. By the mid- and late 2000s – and for the first time since the feminist, Black Arts Movement and identity politics exhibitions of the 1980s (each with its attendant legitimating discourse) politicised art was exhibited in large mainstream exhibitions. In between, neoliberal market discourse took hold in the artworld with Sarah Kent, and later to a lesser extent Matthew Collings, expounding the virtues of the Young British Artists (YBAs) and celebrating their entrepreneurialism. With every shift in the type of artwork exhibited widely within the artworld, there has been an attendant discourse.

Although Kent can be identified as the pre-eminent London critic of the YBAs during the 1990s, the artworld's sudden market-orientation was not the product of one critic or magazine's enthusiasm. We must understand instead that discourse is distributed diffusely. It is not just one critic or philosopher that makes 'art', in Danto's sense. During the 1990s, art historians had started to write about how the avant-garde ideal of maintaining a distance between art and commerce was filled with hubris.[7] Michael Fitzgerald's *Making Modernism: Picasso and the Creation of the Market for Twentieth-Century Art* (1996) may be understood as evidence that avant-garde artists were indeed involved in the market; it may also be understood as evidence that, during the 1990s, there was a sudden proliferation of market-apologist, art-historical writing in addition to the proliferation of market-orientated art.[8] Even the more critical magazines such as *Art Monthly* started to employ the language of market meritocracy at this time and repeated often one of the neoliberal articles of faith that equates populism with democracy. Writing in the same vein was the publication *An Introduction to Aesthetics* (1997) by US philosopher Dabney Townsend, which attempted to make the philosophical case for a 'new' aesthetic formed by the new relationship between mass popular audiences and art-makers.[9] Even one of the most visible critically engaged artists at the turn of the millennium, Carey Young, who engaged with market ideology and discourse, did so, not in political terms but as semiotic and ironic critique. Claire Bishop writes with surprise that in the mid-1990s, curators and artists distanced themselves from any political or social reading of their work.[10] This surprise stems from a lack of understanding about the role of discourse in art. It also betrays a lack of awareness of how much discourse and normative pressures have changed over the past few decades.

The relationship described by Danto between writing and art practice goes against a liberal artworld homily that the category of art is an ever-expanding, progressive one, invariably proceeding from exclusion to inclusion as Wittgenstein's open concept philosophy might allow. The artworld is proud of art's ability to shock whenever there are new, highly visible inclusions into the definition of art. We can think of a parade of shocking incursions made by Marcel Duchamp, Pierre Manzoni, Carl Andre and Tracey Emin to name but a few. In the 1980s there was a widely read tome on the subject by Robert Hughes, published following the BBC television series *The Shock of the New* (1980). But this idea belies an historical reality of constant flux.

It is in the continental philosophical tradition, not the analytic one, that processes of normalisation and legitimation operating to effect changes in discourse are described. Changes occur in the types of discourse considered legitimate, fashionable, apt, 'now', and these changes affect the material conditions for perceiving what is art, what is not art and the value of art as art. Far from being ever expanding and inclusive, the artworld favours one type of practice at one time and another in different circumstances, and writing plays a pivotal role in the process of legitimation as art. Normative language operates so that certain phrases or concerns indicate worldiness or aptness to the moment. Conversely, outmoded notions from which we are supposed to have evolved or which are supposed to have been resolved are also reproduced through normative mechanisms. These are sometimes overt but equally they can be subtle in their pervasiveness.

These processes have been described for science in Bruno Latour's ground-breaking work *Laboratory Life* (1979). He describes how knowledge is formed in the lab through a time-based process of consensus and then amnesia about what was excluded in the process of consensus. His work does not aim at undermining scientific achievement but contextualises scientific knowledge-formation as a social process.[11] This is not how people who do science like to see what they do. Similarly the artworld retains myths about how it operates. The anthropological ethnography of Latour may be understood as producing insight, not only for the scientific laboratory, but for the artworld institution.

This book may attempt to create another artworld discourse, one that answers the problems that have arisen for art specifically since neoliberalism, but there must be a conducive set of conditions for a new paradigm to occur. One article, one book, one exhibition, does not shift discourse unless there are wider operations at work to create the phenomenon of the 'newly current' idea. A clear example of this can be seen in the length of time and processes involved to repoliticise or re-engage the wider London artworld in social and ethical ideas after the 'identity politics' of the 1980s were comprehensively superseded by market-orientated art and discourse. For example, in 1997, artist Liz Ellis wrote an article presenting an ethical challenge to the domination of market-orientated discourse and the YBA phenomenon. It was published by a marginal journal.[12] In the same year, 'Documenta X' (the vast international quinquennial biennial exhibition) was staged in Kassel, drawing on and mostly restaging radical, political and socially engaged projects from the twentieth century. It was 'widely criticised at the time for being a form of outdated left-wing nostalgia', as Gail Day notes.[13] A few years later the 'Protest & Survive' exhibition curated by Matthew Higgs and Paul Noble was held at Whitechapel Art Gallery in 2000, which largely drew on a similar curatorial strategy to 'Documenta X'.[14] It was similarly dismissed as both dated and nostalgic.[15] But the 1999 publication of Julian Stallabrass's *High Art Lite*, a critique of YBA art and its underpinnings, marks a turning point in London artworld discourse and, by the time the English translation of Nicolas Bourriaud's *Relational Aesthetics* (2002) was published, a complete change of direction in artworld discourse had occurred: the London artworld was on the brink of a new acceptability for political, radical art practices. By the time Okwui Enwezor curated the next Documenta, 'Documenta XI', in 2002, with his emphasis on democracy, truth and globalisation, Catherine David's 'Documenta X' was understood retrospectively as 'remarkably prescient'.[16]

Normative processes that structure artworld language may overtly pit an old idea against a newer one, legitimating one set of discourses against another. It may be overtly stated that one type of politics is passé or the issues it raises resolved. Whole types of discourse are also delegitimated by the process of exclusion, as described in the introduction to David Willer's *Network Exchange Theory*:

> Both Marx and Weber recognised exclusion as a condition of structural power. This recognition is significant because exclusion is undoubtedly the single most important structural condition producing power.[17]

It is this type of power, in particular, that the artworld employs collectively. Certain types of ideas, artists and practices may be simply excluded and rendered invisible. Funding may be withheld, such as when the Arts Council of England rescinded funding for Artists Placement Group in the 1990s on the grounds that they did not make art. Exhibition ideas that were prevalent and important in one period may be suddenly hard to stage, invisible, or marginalised.[18] It may be changes in material conditions that create new discourse, or a new visibility for countervailing discourse that already exists. But discourse itself is not the whole picture. Danto is not wholly correct. For example, the rise and fall of the market seems either to foretell or follow changes in discourse and the perception of different types of art practice. The 1990s were boom years for the market. The 1970s were years of recession and the first decade of the 2000s saw both 'capitalism in crisis' and the marked increase in the gap between rich and poor. Perhaps it is no coincidence that political art is in the ascendant when times are bad and market-orientated art reigns in periods of market boom. George Dickie's version of the Institutional definition of art, which looks not to writing about art but to social processes, provides a fuller picture. Dickie helps to explain these artworld variations over time as more than just the product of artworld writing and thinking.

George Dickie and the Institutional definition of art

The Institutional definition of art has another component, emphasising, instead of the centrality of discourse, the social mechanisms operating to create the definition of art. Dickie takes the institutional definition further than Danto would like, concluding with an almost heretical (in philosophy circles) tautology:

- An artist is a person who participates with understanding in the making of a work of art.

- A work of art is an artifact of a kind created to be presented to an artworld public.
- A public is a set of persons the members of which are prepared in some degree to understand an object which is presented to them.
- The artworld is the totality of all artworld systems.
- An artworld system is a framework for the presentation of a work of art by an artist to an artworld public.[19]

The consequence of Dickie's ideas is that anything the artworld says is art *is* art. There are no criteria other than artworld consensus. That this is true is evidenced in the many artworks that hinge on the idea of an artistic 'Midas touch'. Examples of objects becoming art on an artist's say-so range from Carl Andre's *Equivalent VIII* (1966) (the infamous pile of 120 firebricks in rectangular configuration, two piles of 60 bricks laid longwise in 6 x 10 arrangement) to what can be understood as its next generation reprise, Martin Creed's artwork, like, for example, the blob of Blu-Tack, *Work No. 79* (1993). Clearly, at least some artists have an art practice that centres on employing the very slippages and inherent shock-value that this definition of art allows, self-consciously manipulating the power to legitimate objects as art. Jeremy Deller and Alan Kane's *Folk Archive* (1999 ongoing) seems to reflect on that gift. The artwork is the curation and display of the kind of objects and practice that have been excluded from contemporary art galleries. The archive includes traditional folk crafts and working-class art and craft objects: the very objects dismissed by Clement Greenberg in his 'Art and Kitsch' essay. Neither Deller nor Kane describes their work as a reflection on, or intervention into, the Institutional definition of art. Instead,

> *Folk Archive* is an attempt to explore and document such creativity in Britain and Ireland with the aim of celebrating the diversity of these significant cultural activities. *An*

> *introduction to Folk archive* ... presents for the first time a few examples of the artists' findings during a year-long search across Britain. These include, for instance, meticulously crafted objects obtained from Women's Institute bazaars, photographs and video footage documenting fairs, Morris dancing, political demonstrations and performative practices such as tattooing.[20]

Folk Archive performs the power to legitimate as 'art'. The artefacts in *Folk Archive* would ordinarily be overlooked by the artworld but in the hands of artists, reframing those particular objects within the gallery setting, the totality of the objects, and perhaps the objects themselves, become art. In this work, Deller and Kane perform what is implied by Dickie's Institutional Theory of Art: the act of transformation. For Jacques Rancière, a philosopher in the continental tradition, it is this act of transformation that is at the heart of Romanticism.[21] *Brillo Boxes, Equivalent VIII* and *Folk Archive* can be seen as simply the logical extension of an aesthetic philosophy, namely Romanticism, which rendered the boundary of art permeable; a discourse through which the prosaic readily became elevated to the status of art, as objects worthy of aesthetic contemplation.

Of the philosophical contributions described here, it is Dickie who most closely describes the reality of the contemporary artworld because he describes how only some objects become art even if any object might. His idea is that, through this conferral of status, a given object becomes 'art'. Art is not something that exists outside this process. The implication of his theory is that art is made through a consensus of people with the power to define what is art.[22] He makes no judgements about this process. It is a 'value-neutral' theory. That is, this process is not to be understood as either a good thing or a bad thing. Some philosophers, including (perhaps surprisingly) Danto, have argued against Dickie's theory, believing that there is no such group of people with institutionalising power. *Folk Archive*, or *Folk Archive* in the context of Tate Britain, indicates otherwise. For an analytic philosopher to conclude with such a social idea is heretical. Coming to his defence, another analytic philosopher, Robert Yanal, writes that, 'if "art" can only be defined in terms of social practice, then this may just be a brute fact about the concept of art, not an objection to the institutional theory'.[23]

It is precisely for this reason that Dickie's philosophy is useful here, because even in the abstract – considered divorced from any specific historical and geographical circumstances – the very definition of art must be understood as being determined by a social process. There is no quality, there is nothing else that defines art. If art, or, more precisely, art as it is defined at all times and in all circumstances, has as its very definition that it can only be defined in terms of social practice, then we in the artworld must look hard at what that means. We determine what is and what is not art. We do this collectively. One individual does not define art but all the individuals in the artworld collectively define art. Another way of saying this is that, as artists, we maintain and police the boundaries of art, by definition. We do this with our theories and our practice. Further, in defining art and policing its boundaries we also create its values.

In recent years, not only has the definition of art changed (in keeping with the Institutional theory), but even since Danto's 1964 text, the definition of art has both accommodated and expelled a variety of practices, including both the highly commercial and the highly political. The definition of art has not only shifted, it has contracted over time, which means that depending on discursive and structural changes within the artworld, artists have found their work either inside or outside its definition. Both the overtly politically orientated and the overtly commercially orientated have at various times throughout the twentieth century been illegitimate, or not-art, within the artworld Institutional definition of art. As described above, with the new millennium, politicised or activist practice was reintroduced as a legitimate art practice in the UK for the first time since the late 1980s, although a notable exception was made during the 1990s for those artists whose backgrounds were expected to be 'political', fulfilling Western stereotypes, such as those from Latin America, China and Russia. Notably, at the time there was also a growing market for art from these places.[24] By contrast, the artists working in the leftist tradition in the UK and US at that time became marginalised or invisible, as described by the eminent leftist US artist Martha Rosler in a 1998 interview.[25] There has been a corresponding waxing and waning in credibility for overtly commercially orientated art during the post-war period, as demonstrated by the fall in Warhol's artworld credibility in the 1970s and 1980s and his subsequent reinstatement as artworld great in the 1990s.[26] One of the points of the discipline of history is to remind us of this waxing and waning because, without historical insight, we tend to forget that the past was different. We have a tendency to imagine that present conditions and assumptions have always been thus.[27]

It is worth noting that the contemporary artworld still has limits as to what is considered art. The artworld's rejection of the paintings of Jack Vettriano as art, despite him being the best-selling painter in Britain, seems to indicate that there remains limits to the inclusion of the highly commercial within the artworld, but this may change.[28] What counts as legitimate art practice is specific to its moment in time and space and relies on a range of legitimating factors. Each of us is part of that process. The issue of the Institutional definition of art is one of validity or legitimacy. Sociologist Pascal Gielen applied actor-network theory to the artworld in order to describe how curators from different generations created networks within the artworld, positioning themselves as legitimators of art and artists.[29] Gielen's analysis may imply power in the hands of a select few and power *is* distributed variably across the artworld. But in another sense, power is more widely distributed as well: whether or not Jan Hoet and Barbara Vanderlinden (the examples he cites) are widely accepted as interesting or relevant curator-directors is down to a broader artworld consensus.

If there are no criteria other than artworld consensus, the definition of art must therefore be understood in thoroughly social-political terms. By implicating a social dimension within the very definition of art, Dickie's philosophy seems to dovetail into the observations of Pierre Bourdieu. For Bourdieu, art has primarily a social-political function. It is a mechanism of social distinction, an effective tool for establishing bourgeois modalities and dominance. The consumption of art and high culture is one of the means by which the middle and upper classes distinguish themselves from the rest of society. In short, for Bourdieu, art is to signify distinctions in class.[30] From the point of view of the artworld, though, some art does this but art is much more than this as well.

What art does is determined by artworld consensus. Historically, there were 'alternatives' to the rarefied and monied part of the artworld: spaces (either official or unofficial, funded or otherwise) and discourses that were different from the market and the state-sponsored. It was only in the 2000s that large numbers of artists in the London artworld, including those with leftist and radical politics, began to notice what happened at the biennials, started taking league tables seriously and government funding as a sign of legitimacy.

Conclusion

The relationship of art to class and commerce is complex – far more complex than most historians suggest. Art historian Oskar Bätschmann observed that an ambivalence towards commerce was present at the start of the modern period, as part of an Enlightenment renegotiation regarding the purpose of art within the new world order.[31] While it is important to realise how class is implicated in art, it is also important to realise how class is implicated in the very definition of art. Class here may mean monied or upper- and middle-class, as Bourdieu uses it, but class may also mean type. As a class of people, artists, curators and others in the artworld collectively define art and its value. This may or may not revolve around the tastes and discourse of the monied class.

Rather than an open, free and autonomous world of creative and intellectual expression, we must understand that the artworld is governed by regulating concepts and networks of power that operate under myths of freedom and autonomy serving to obscure its operations. It seems we, as constituents of the artworld, are both subject to discourse and create discourse, as this frames what we do as artists. Discourse frames whether or not what we do is legitimate as art. Put like this, it becomes obvious that the artworld is metonymic of power as it operates more generally in society. The next chapter looks at models of power as they have been perceived historically, and more or less how they continue to be perceived within the artworld today. It then offers a different model of power as described by Michel Foucault which, though often cited within the artworld, seems not to inform our behaviour, individually and collectively, as constitutive of both the artworld and wider society.

Part II
Artworld Orthodoxies

Having established (1) that the contemporary artworld replicates neoliberal structures and values, and (2) that what comprises art is determined by discourse and the consensus of artworld constituents and nothing else, by definition, I will now turn to two historical debates that dog contemporary art practice and prevent true radicalism. The argument in Part II of this book is that artists on the left, those who are interested in resistance, have unwittingly allowed neoliberalism to inform our values through a lack of awareness of the history of artworld thought or by uncritically accepting its legacy. We have not recognised that structures of power, including artworld structures, have radically altered since the 2000s, and we have altered ourselves to fit these neoliberal structures without realising it. Artistic ambitions are eclipsed by neoliberal ones and, because we have no distinct values with which to negotiate neoliberalism, we fail to resist or even to recognise where we do not resist. In addition, though the artworld cites nuanced theories of power, most still model the world in simplistic binaries, such as powerful and powerless. Chapter 4 describes another distraction that has allowed us to embrace market norms unwittingly, namely the art–life binary, from which a set of assumptions about what makes an art practice political has been established. We have inherited the assumption that one type of art practice is inherently radical, political, critical or anti-market and that this is the only language in which to make critical, ethical or political art. The arguments in Part II are that art fails as a potential site of resistance because artists fail to understand the nature of power and our place within it, and because we are thwarted by ideas of authentic resistance.

CHAPTER 3
Understanding Power

Summary

In general, political artists or artists working with a community-based, dialogic, activist or self-consciously ethical practice tend to work within a particular model of power, which can be described as a binary model. In the binary model of power, the world is divided into categories: powerful–powerless, good–bad, us–them. Art practices that are based on this framework work within a set of assumptions imagining that power is located within a specific group of people or a specific set of institutions. This model of power does not recognise the subtleties and nuances within the processes and techniques of power. It either imagines others as powerful while we ourselves are powerless, or it imagines others as powerless and only we have the power to help. In itself, this is simplistic and it is offensive. In terms of art practice, it is also limiting and disabling. We too may reproduce the injustices and inequalities of power, exploiting and excluding in precisely the same way that wider mechanisms of power operate; we may ourselves act in ways that embody power relations and end up replicating and supporting what we wish to critique. The binary model of power contains a number of problematic concepts that, in addition to being reductive and misleading, constrain art practice. The ideas of false consciousness, authenticity and recuperation or co-optation are the product of a binary model that sees good–bad and powerful–powerless in either/or terms. This chapter describes theories of power that are more nuanced and complex than this, implicating ourselves as agents and as part of the mechanisms of power. It could be argued that the model of power described here is a Foucauldian perspective on Dickie's observations about the Institutional definition of art: each of us is constitutive, doing our own policing, by definition, rather than simply subject. The chapter asks that we first recognise the nature of power if, in fact, we are interested in resisting it; that we move from a binary model, which affords only ineffectual action, to a complex model of power in order to disrupt, subvert or enact other values.

◆ ◆ ◆ ◆

This chapter in particular is written in response to my experience of creatively inspired activists over 2009 and since. Reflection on that experience then threw a new light on the practices of those artists who are politicised or socially engaged. Both groups inevitably address issues of power within their work.

Within the artworld, we have for decades referred to the 'carceral continuum' or 'archaeologies of knowledge' theorised by Foucault, which describe how our very bodies, desires and knowledge are sites for the reproduction of power – and yet somehow the reductive binary model of power continues to have an evergreen appeal. Despite the fact that Foucault has been on reading lists consistently since the late 1980s, it is the older, more simplistic models of power that inform nearly all types of art practice (and activism). In this chapter I first describe the simplistic view of power most often imagined by practitioners within the artworld, one that is set up in binary terms (us–them, powerful–powerless, good–bad), and then explore the theory that mechanisms of power implicate us all, drawing on Foucault.

A Marxist understanding of the power-culture nexus was the mainstay of an art education from the 1970s until the early 1990s, and although this is no longer regularly taught in art colleges, the argument here is that certain assumptions, which are the product of that legacy, abound in the contemporary artworld about the nature of power and dissent.

In thinking about the continuing appeal of binaries for the artworld, it could be argued that the history of art and the avant-garde has been described in binary terms since the dawn of modernity. Binaries lie at the heart of the telling of art history and the theories that motivate or surround artists' practices. With the advent of modernity, and well before the historical avant-garde, came the notion of artistic freedom. This was understood as an integral value to an artistic practice; it was contrasted from the beginning with the *unfreedom* of institutions, the state or the bourgeoisie, as Bätschmann describes.[1] A particular reading of Immanuel Kant has the division of the aesthetic realm from the realm of life and, following this schema, the artworld has subsequently imagined an inherent tension between art and life, aesthetics and ethics. From the late nineteenth century and throughout the twentieth, binaries at the heart of artistic practice revolved around the idea of the avant-garde. In a process termed negation, or defining one's practice against something, the avant-garde set up a range of straw men against which to create. Gail Day writes:

> 'Negation' is part of the routine language of art, and arguments about negativity are thoroughly embedded in accounts of culture and the debates on modernity and avant-gardism – and, by implication, those on postmodernity, or on the neo-avant-gardes and post-avant-gardes – frequently serving as vehicles for these discussions.[2]

Past norms, the mainstream, the public, 'life', commerce, the Academy: these are all objects of negation against which artists of the avant-garde have chosen to respond. Arguably, the binary model of power that most artists today continue to imagine when they conceive their art practice persists because of this long formative history of negation. Many disparate theorists on contemporary art, including Johanna Drucker, Boris Groys and Jacques Rancière, have been calling for an end to simplistic binaries as the model for a politics of dissent. But binaries appear to be too integral to the artworld to be easily displaced and their very simplicity has an ongoing seduction. Ironically, although the futility of artists working within this model is described in Drucker's *Sweet Dreams: Contemporary Art and Complicity* (2005) and in Boris Groys' *Art Power* (2008), both authors continue to work within them. Both advocate an art practice that 'uses' existing artworld market mechanisms, as distinct from working from a position that is imagined to be 'outside' or in opposition. For Drucker and Groys, there is subversive potential, politically, in working knowingly and directly within the mechanisms of the market system. Their emphasis is that this is more interesting and more aesthetically pleasing than inhabiting *the alternative.* Their version of the 'third way' comes from reading Foucault through the traditional artworld politics of binary. There is the market, there is its opposite, and then there is what they advocate: bringing the alternative into the market mainstream and abandoning the idea of alternatives. I would argue that their third way position stems from a misunderstanding both of how neoliberalism has changed artworld structures in the first place, and a misreading of Foucault, whose work insists there is no *a priori* outside position within society or discourse. The 'alternative' is always already part of the artworld and society.

This chapter takes us from the reductive binary model and the problems that arise from working within it, to the more subtle model of power that implicates each of us, not simply because it is more correct, but because unless we understand how power operates in reality we will inevitably replicate the structures, norms and values of neoliberalism, even when our personal politics or ethics run counter.

Models of power

Marxist theorist Antonio Gramsci (1891–1937) wrote between 1926 and the 1930s when he was imprisoned on charges fabricated by Italy's Fascist government. His critique of power describes how values are created in society through various 'educative outlets' such as museums and the media, and also the hegemonic investment in this process that supports power held in the hands of a few. Few of us working in the media, museums and galleries like to imagine our work in these terms, yet nearly a century on there is continuing perspicacity in Gramsci's theory of power, as Tony Bennett observes.[3] With the rise of neoliberalism, market mechanisms and market-orientated normative discourse inform nearly every sphere and social–cultural organisation, including the artworld, and it can no longer be seen as accurate (if ever it was) to describe the political–cultural milieu of the UK in terms of dichotomy. Even in 1933 Gramsci wrote that this is too simplistic a view of power. I would add that the continued persistence of the simplistic binary is fuelled by our desire to locate power elsewhere and to operate by negation.[4]

Changing from binaries

It is evident that a number of changes have occurred with neoliberalism that leave any notion of a binary model of power in tatters. Traditional distinctions became interwoven and whole categories became irrelevant. For example, since the 1990s, centre-left governments of both the UK and the US entrenched economic policies that undermined separate public and private sectors and the idea of distinct, traditional classes. Under the New Labour government (1997–2010) the concept of class was replaced by a rhetoric of inclusion and policies of 'self-responsibilisation', a technique of self-management described by Foucault.[5] The working-class/upper-class binary was rhetorically, if not actually, dismantled and so too was the market-state binary with state integration of the market through privatisation, the 'mixed-economy' and other public–private finance initiatives.

Once a neoliberal policy of right-wing governments, state-private integration was adopted by the left, not only for pragmatic reasons as was generally portrayed at the time, but for ideological ones as well, as Anthony Giddens (author of *The Third Way*) writes.[6] Further, according to political theorist Alex Callinicos, Tony Blair had a 'sincere belief that the public sector is best run by private enterprise'.[7] The succeeding Conservative–Liberal Democrat coalition government from 2010 returned rhetoric to binaries on public–private lines, demonstrating the seductiveness of binaries in traditional politics. This time the public–private binary served as a rhetorical distraction from the fact that successive UK governments since 1979 had entrenched neoliberal mechanisms and values, rendering distinctions between the sectors minimal. After all, it was Gordon Brown who shared with Milton Friedman, the influential economist whose theories underpin neoliberalism, the idea that:

> If macro-economic stability is secured and the right supply-side measures are in place, any further unemployment is voluntary. Unemployment is in these circumstances a consequence of the dysfunctional behaviour of individuals who refuse to work, and this behaviour must in turn be caused either by their individual moral faults or by a more pervasive 'culture of poverty'.[8]

In other words, it is not a systemic failure that causes unemployment (under conditions of market growth), but individual failure. Neoliberal ideology looks to individuals, rather than systems, for the causes of social ills.

Changing the artworld

Translating these ideas to the artworld, within neoliberal ideology it is not the system that is at fault if an artist fails to find a market but the fault of the individual artist. As Chapter 2 demonstrated, this is true: if the artworld is neoliberal in its structures and values, all instances of success and failure are down to the individual's ability to work within these values. This seems to be an implication of the Institutional definition of art. A different implication is that if the artworld operates with values other than neoliberal ones, then artists are no longer to be judged with reference to neoliberalism. Failure to find a market is no longer failure in artistic terms.

With the neoliberal structural changes that successive governments since Thatcher have implemented, concurrent structural changes have taken place within the museums and galleries sector. In addition to those described in Chapter 1, there are those analysed by Chin-tao Wu in *Privatising Culture: Corporate Art Intervention since the 1980s* (2002). Charting the rise of corporate involvement in individual museums in the UK and US, and how individuals working in those museums came to incorporate corporate values at the heart of museum practice, her research is a meticulous record of the rise and dominance of neoliberal mechanisms and values within the artworld,[9] documenting the changes that occurred over this period to privatise the arts.

While it is true that critique did exist in artworld institutions over this period, it was in the form of institutional critique, which tends to posit a binary model of victims and villains (although more subtle forms of institutional critique also exist, such as Tino Sehgal's 'This Success or This Failure' (2007) ICA, London). Despite this, it is clear that the artworld assumes that current structures are good for art, benign, or at least don't matter. If this were not true, collectively we would be creating other structures, discourses and art.

Art and commerce

Primarily concerned with changes in capitalism and not in the artworld, Ève Chiapello and Luc Boltanski chart the beginning of the relationship between art and commerce from another point in the twentieth century. In *The New Spirit of Capitalism* (1999 [2004 English translation]), they analysed 'management literature' and its relationship to capitalism; their research charts the evolution of discourse within capitalism and the evolution of its mechanisms. According to their thesis, in response to the events of May 1968, capitalism became 'artistic'. In other words, capitalism acquired the values intrinsic to art, namely freedom and self-expression – values reiterated in management literature and reproduced widely. There was a convergence of artistic values with capitalist ones, and the new hybrid dominated thinking, not only in business but in the artworld, both at the level of elite galleries and national museums, and across all parts of the publicly funded sector including the radical end of the spectrum.

Structural changes occurring with the rise of neoliberalism have affected the structures of the artworld, and the artworld itself has altered and accommodated them. In addition, the values of art have been so aligned with neoliberalism as to mean that any artistic practice originating in notions of self-expression and freedom replicates its norms and values. Yet the artworld operates as if these changes haven't happened, as if the model of power and discourse that sustained ideas of avant-garde negation still existed. I will argue instead for a more nuanced conception of power, one implicating us as agents, just as neoliberalism does, as an important conceptual leap. In Foucault's words:

> [individuals] effect by their own means or with the help of others a certain number of operations on their own bodies and souls, thoughts, conduct, and way of being, so as to transform themselves in order to attain a certain state of happiness, purity, wisdom, perfection, or immortality.[10]

In other words, we are our own agents of power. We produce and reproduce domination of our own free will, on and through our own bodies, in order to achieve social and personal goals.

Problems for art and activism produced by a binary model of power

The avant-garde tradition imagines power in binary terms of powerful–powerless or ruling-class–proletariat and the antagonism between hegemonic ideology that serves ruling-class privilege pitted against a countervailing culture rising from the conditions of the subordinated popular classes. This type of simplistic Marxist conception of power includes ideas of authenticity, the notion of recuperation or co-optation and 'false consciousness'. Whether or not the artworld acknowledges it, this is the model of power most often imagined. Most exhibitions and conferences that purport an ethical, radical or politicised position, do so from within an imagined dichotomy in which an imagined *they* have all the power and *we* have all the answers.

One of the ideas that come from a binary Marxist tradition, has it that the ruling class produces discourse that is distinct from our needs, where reality is cynically manufactured so that our desires are created, mollifying us to accept our place in the status quo or bamboozling our 'real needs' with false desires for commodities, or status, or Coca-Cola. This binary model of power has it that we passively receive as truth the discourse generated by the ruling elite.

False consciousness

The idea of 'false consciousness' is associated mostly with Marxist theorist Georg Lukács and is an attempt at theorising why the subordinated classes make choices that are ultimately against their best interest. An example would be those working in poor conditions for little pay but doing nothing to alter those conditions. Marxist theorists, surprised by the lack of revolutionary spirit evinced by the masses throughout the twentieth century, explained this as the product of false consciousness. Consequently, 'consciousness-raising', or education and agitprop, became a strategy towards revolution. We can see these same assumptions flavouring some types of contemporary art practice. It had been assumed that all that was needed was for the masses to understand the situation (as Marxists saw it) and so class revolution, leading to equality for all, would commence.

Many social movements, including feminism, have worked with these assumptions and held 'consciousness-raising' events. The successes of feminism could be seen as evidence for false consciousness and the efficacy of promoting a feminist consciousness, but there are also other ways of explaining its success. A concurrent general change in discourse may have included consciousness-raising events and activities that were a manifestation of these larger and more diffuse discursive changes. In other words, they were manifestation not catalyst. The limits to the ongoing success of feminism indicate the difficulty in overcoming entrenched problems that are not felt to be subsequent of falsely held views. The ongoing gender pay-gap, difficulties in the prosecution of rape and, in the artworld, the under-representation and under-valuation of women artists, are problems that are understood to exist but understanding them as problematic hasn't produced a change in these areas.

Objections to the assumptions within the idea of false consciousness come from both the left and the right, including the criticism that it is an inherently patronising view of the masses: that *they* (the masses) don't know what is good for them but *we* (the artists, the thinkers) do. Art based on the idea of consciousness-raising also assumes a debunked pedagogical model by which students are imagined as empty buckets to be filled by expert knowledge; that art can 'teach' in this sense. As early as 1760 Jean Jacques Rousseau had already described problems with the pedagogical model of art. He understood that art can never be politically or pedagogically efficacious because representation entails a separation between seeing and doing.[11] Jacques Rancière described this in *Dissensus: On Politics and Aesthetics*:

> Critical art is an art that aims to produce a new perception of the world, and therefore to create a commitment to its transformation. This schema, very simple in appearance, is actually the conjunction of three processes: first, the production of a sensory form of 'strangeness'; second, the development of an awareness of the reason for that strangeness and third, a mobilization of individuals as a result of that awareness.[12]

He goes on to discuss that, in eliding these three processes, the notion that awareness of an injustice or a problem will necessarily motivate people to act is fostered. Awareness of environmental damage is a case in point: of those who are recently convinced of anthropogenic climate change some appear disabled by this new understanding, acting exactly as they have always done despite understanding the human impact on global climate. This may be because they don't want to think about it, it is too enormous an issue, or it puts too great or too little an emphasis on their individual action in their own understanding. The fact remains that many who are convinced of our impact on the climate still fail to make the changes deemed necessary to slow or alter this process. Simplistic models cannot account for the complexity of human thought and behaviour, as both individuals and as groups, and it is a mistake to base an art practice on such a reductive understanding of our collective needs, desires, knowledges.

Critical pedagogy

One answer to the various criticisms against pedagogic art comes in the form of popular education or critical pedagogy as described by Paolo Freire, whose theory is cited both by activists and by the artworld.[13] For Freire, the 'fundamental objective [of education] is to fight alongside the people for the recovery of the people's stolen humanity'.[14] Many contemporary artists working within the avant-garde tradition find this attractive, understanding that art is itself fundamental to recovering people's 'stolen humanity'. Despite reference to Freire's methodologies, there is a continuing tension in much of this type of art practice. Freire's is the collaborative model of democratic participation *par excellence* and his approach puts centrally the goals that a community decides on. Importantly, the focus is the goals and approaches that come from the community and their experience and not those that are understood from the outside as being in the community's best interest. Where artists have an artistic agenda, or activists a political agenda, they will impose it even when working collaboratively with communities and even when there is an awareness of, and respect for, Freire's ideas. Any outside political, educational or aesthetic agenda is fundamentally incompatible with Freire's democratic, community-originated and context-specific pedagogic methodology. A methodological tension arises when an artist both has an agenda but also wants to follow Freire's pedagogical model for working with communities. Embedded power relations dictate that the artist has power, knowledge, status or resources that the community doesn't have. Interesting art may result from the tension, or in spite of it, but what is pertinent here is the embedded power relations between artist and participant, which are often disavowed disingenuously.

Authenticity and recuperation

The binary idea of power fosters other inherent problems for radical or political art practice, namely the idea of authenticity and co-optation or recuperation. Although arguments against imagining power in binary terms have been around for a few decades, the idea of recuperation still has currency, as was seen in the Arnolfini gallery's journal *Art, Activism, Recuperation* (2009). The spectre of recuperation demands that all forms of critique or resistance occur 'outside' or in other imagined spaces of authentic resistance. Where the artworld imagines an inside–outside, good–bad dichotomy, artworks and exhibitions are applauded or dismissed simply because of where they are situated within artworld structures. Authentic sites of resistance and authentic voices are produced. Modelling power in binary terms disavows the agency of those who are 'inauthentically' sited, creating sometimes absurd tensions such as the idea that only *this* oppressed person can speak about oppression, whereas a person who is oppressed differently or apparently not at all may not speak about oppressive structures or regimes. This is not just untenable theoretically but, more importantly, from the point of view of art and activism it is inherently disempowering to most forms of resistance as it has the potential to disavow nearly any action, any method and any voice when deemed to be on the wrong side of binary categorisation. Importantly, it also fails to recognise genuine resistance, because resistance is compelled to appear in certain sanctioned ways. Finally, within the model of authenticity and recuperation, created as a product of a binary model of power and determining what is deemed inherently good or bad art, lies the good or bad, appropriate or inappropriate methods or media of the politically engaged artist. Parts of the next chapter are devoted to the problems that arise from this binary to disable the potential for art based on whole clusters of good–bad artistic practices, display and media.

Dialectics

Before I attempt to describe a non-binary model of power, I address one last inheritance for the artworld of the Marxist model, namely dialectics. Many in the Marxist tradition are inspired by Hegel's philosophy of history, describing the master–slave dialectic, and so view class struggle in terms of a dialectic: a dynamic tussle between two classes of things, namely the powerful and powerless (struggles for power in 'race' and gender terms have also been understood as a dialectic). This struggle ends, according to Hegel, when the slave, revelling in his true unalienated labour, becomes whole and the master by contrast becomes weak, being wholly dependent on the slave. As differences between slave and master are dissolved, both recognise that they are interdependent, so the struggle ends.

Following Hegel, Marxist thinkers share as central precepts the idea of a dialectical struggle. One way of reading the victories of feminism described above would be in terms of dialectics: that there was a dialectical struggle between patriarchy (the right of men to dominate women) and feminism (the right of women to be perceived and treated as equal to men) and an accommodation between the two has been made. Feminists have as our goal full equality, whereas those who support the norms of patriarchy would prefer a reversion to laws that place women under the guardianship of men, usually husbands, fathers and brothers.

An argument against the dialectical view of history and action is made by political theorist Chantal Mouffe, who argues that once the idea of stable and fixed identities, meanings or transcendent values were undermined through post-structural critique, the seeming certainties that sustain the dialectical model broke down. She explains that by helping us to 'abandon the abstract universalism of the Enlightenment, the essentialist conception of a social totality, and the myth of a unitary subject, a project of radical and plural democracy' could emerge. A radical and plural democracy requires 'the existence of multiplicity, of plurality and of conflict, and sees them as the *raison d'être* of politics'.[15] By its very nature a dialectical model cannot accommodate plurality as it requires two classes of things. In other words, the idea of dialectics has an inherent homogenising tendency because it is between *two* things. To reduce the complexity of power and its operations to two classes, diametrically opposed, will inevitably further marginalise and disempower some within those groups and usually the most vulnerable.

Further, a dialectic imagines a forward march, a progression, and this idea is also problematic. Philosopher and historian R. G. Collingwood argues that the type of historical storytelling that imposes on history a unifying narrative structure does a disservice to historical reality. Like any other story of progress, dialectical struggle is teleological, explaining the present as if it is the project of the past to evolve into it. Yet clearly, like the present, when the past was the present, it operated for itself, with its own motivations and not in respect of an inherently unknowable future. Further, Collingwood argues that history is most often used as a type of self-portrait. We imagine ourselves reflected in the past, writing histories that are in fact accounts of the present refracted through what we choose to see or know about the past.[16]

The idea of history that underpins this book echoes Collingwood's view. The present is not understood as the product of a dialectical struggle but the product of discourse and structures. Similar ideas have stemmed from postmodern thought and have been dismissed for their apolitical narration of historical structures. I acknowledge the importance of the idea of continuous struggle to Marxist thought but reject the teleological view that addresses itself to a revolutionary future. Viewing the present as a specific moment in time and space with various constraints and structures that exist, each of us is freed and compelled to act in this moment because it is *this* moment that is under construction.

Not all Marxists base their politics in the idea of dialectical struggle, and others, who do favour a dialectical model, do not necessarily imagine it in reductive binary terms. It is activists and artists who tend to find the binary appealing and useful. Alex Callinicos writes in *Against the Third Way: An Anti-Capitalist Critique*:

> Only in the most vulgar leftist (or in fact fascist) critiques do a handful of monopolists get together to pull the strings. Capitalist firms are necessarily involved in a structure of conflictual interdependence that they cannot individually or even collectively dominate.[17]

He later goes on to explain that Marx himself understood capital as a relation, not a thing, so emphasising that – as a relational entity – there is no inside–outside, us–them terms:

> There is ... a tendency among anti-capitalists to conceive global capitalism as a malign conspiracy. This is personified in the multinationals which are often portrayed, rather like

the Borg in *Star Trek*, as a vast alien entity, constantly on the move, seeking to assimilate and to destroy.[18]

Power is too often understood in binary terms within the artworld, a view that distorts and limits our potential to resist mechanisms of power as they are actually operating. Understanding Foucault's model of power enables us to intervene into neoliberal power as it operates, instead of as it is imagined to operate. In the first place, power is relational. Foucault writes: 'the network of power relations ends by forming a dense web that passes through apparatuses and institutions, without being exactly localized in them'.[19]

A relational understanding of power: Foucault

Within the history of philosophy, Foucault is understood as successor to Existentialism, a term that covers a range of philosophies that converge on the idea that meaning – the meaning of life – does not come from God or religion, as had been the dominant idea for centuries, but lies with the individual taking sole responsibility for life's meaning. For Kierkegaard, that includes living life passionately and sincerely. For Jean-Paul Sartre it means this and, in addition, taking responsibility for one's freedom in one's time. In *Being and Nothingness*, Sartre writes:

> Thus [I am], totally free, undistinguishable from the period for which I have chosen to be the meaning ... The one who realises in anguish his condition as being thrown into a responsibility which extends to his very abandonment has no longer either remorse or regret or excuse; he is no longer anything but a freedom which perfectly reveals itself and whose being resides in this very revelation.[20]

According to Sartre, we are our authentic selves when we choose freedom, the freedom to create meaning in our own lives, in respect of no law, no religion, no authority but ourselves. Sartre maintained that all individuals have freedom, even in response to totalitarianism, those regimes that offer no alternative. Sartre also believed that we can only be authentic if, at the same time as we choose our own freedom, we choose the freedom of others. Authenticity requires each of us to act for everyone's freedom. This is no less true in a world of scarcity and oppression. For Sartre, it is for reasons of bad faith that individuals may not face up to this reality; freedom carries with it a heavy burden. Freedom may produce a deep anguish in ourselves when we understand it.

For Foucault, however, the idea of an authentic self is a fallacy. Clearly, the idea of authenticity predicates a binary model of power as it lies in contradistinction to inauthenticity. Foucault cites instead another Existentialist, Friedrich Nietzsche, and his idea of the self as multiple and therefore an act of creation as a starting point.[21] Because individuals are never exhaustively constructed from the forces of power, there is space within which to question and alter subjectivity. Foucault writes that 'we have to imagine and build up what we could be to get rid of this kind of political "double bind", which is the simultaneous individualization and totalization of modern power structures'.[22]

With regard to the idea of truth and the self, as Kevin Craig Boileau explains, Foucault does not actually get rid of the notion of truth, but instead uses 'the mechanisms of revolt as a process of thought that reveals the contingencies of history in order to determine the possibilities of surpassing current restrictions of the self'.[23] This strategy is in contradistinction to Marxist or Sartrean humanist attempts to uncover a Truth, meaning a true self.

But it is in Sartre's later work, *Critique of Dialectical Reason,* that his understanding of the intersection between the individual and wider society meets that of Foucault's. This work explores the possibility of positive social relations where 'authentic existence' requires some kind of common action on behalf of everyone in a community. True social reciprocity means that we must try to effect changes in the socio-economic conditions that mediate our reciprocity. For Foucault, power is productive not repressive and, because thought has its analogue in action, freedom always involves a set of behavioural choices available in a specific social setting. Power relations are always unstable and capable of being transformed through critical reflection and action.[24]

There is a tendency to read Foucault's analysis of power as nihilistic, or complicit, precisely because it is not dualistic or antagonistic. For some political theorists it is the absence of a binary that renders his theory of power as not-political but this is to misunderstand the model of power he describes. 'Power is less a confrontation between two adversaries', Foucault writes, 'than a question of government'. Instead of primarily using violence for its ends, government establishes unquestioned and accepted ways of thinking, limiting the range, choice, thought and behaviour of individuals.[25] In 'Practising Criticism', Foucault notes that: 'As soon as one can no longer think things as one formerly thought them, transformation becomes both very urgent, very difficult, and quite possible.'[26] In fact, Foucault sees resistance everywhere: wherever there is power there is resistance 'and yet, or rather consequently, this resistance is never in a position of exteriority in relation to power'.[27] There is no outside.

This idea of resistance is not to be mistaken for the idea of resistance as a reaction to, or a negative form of, power; a negation. In no sense does Foucault's concept of power and resistance mimic the binary model of power. Instead, resistance is to be understood as heterogeneous, in the way that art theorist Gerald Raunig describes it:

> a multiplicity of points, nodes, focuses of resistance, not as radical break at the one site, not as a massive disruption that (re)establishes two fundamental oppositions, but as an

unevenly distributed multitude of points of resistance in an equally diverse landscape of shifting splits and boundaries.[28]

A history of other resistance

It is possible to find examples of this type of resistance, as opposed to the overtly revolutionary act, throughout history, including within the British imperial project. Though many have understood this period within the binary model of power, exemplifying a process of domination and repression, it is also possible to view in its history the many Foucauldian acts of resistance. These resistances may have been conscious political acts but they also enact resistance at another register altogether.

Nicholas Thomas, through his anthropological work looking historically at the cultures of the Pacific, argues that global economies and colonialism do not simply impose a homogeneous oppressive schema on all that has gone before, transforming it wholesale in its own image and operating according to binary models of power. The processes of colonialism did not simply obliterate all cultures everywhere, nor act through simple forces imagined within a powerful–powerless dichotomy, but always in relation to the specificities of culture and location. This is not to underestimate the extraordinary violence that was manifested with colonial rule or the obliteration of peoples directly through mass murder, or indirectly through displacement with the forcible acquisition of resources such as land and water, or the inadvertent depopulation of an area through disease. Power operates in relation to individual local systems and values, replicating and matching existing ideas about how to attain, in Foucault's words, 'happiness, purity, wisdom, perfection, or immortality'.[29] The colonial projects of, specifically, capitalism and Christianity only succeeded when overlaid on existing local, native equivalents. Where there were no correlating systems, if no similar trade or symbolic conditions existed locally, then exogenous novel mechanisms and processes such as wage labour, foreign rule or colonial hierarchy failed to take hold. The history revealed by Thomas recognises that the ideas and projects of pre-colonial cultures are a significant factor in the successes or failures of the various aspects of the colonial project.[30]

A type of resistance is also demonstrated in Thomas's analysis of material culture when transported and translated from one context to another:

> As socially and culturally salient entities, objects change in defiance of their material stability. The category to which a thing belongs, the emotion and judgement it prompts, the narrative it recalls, are all historically prefigured. What was English or French in becoming Inuit, is reconstructed socially through indigenous categorisation; similarly, what was Igbo or Javanese, in becoming American or Australian, now conveys something of our projects in foreign places and our aesthetics – something which effaces the intentions of the thing's producers. ... Global economies do not control the meanings of commodities that their profits turn upon, even if the appropriation of these goods in the form of gifts, commodities or prestige valuables inevitably entangles receivers in wider relations that are not easily shrugged off.[31]

In other words, as much as material objects are stable, the discourse that makes sense of them is not. A symmetry exists in the translation of objects from colonising culture to colonised culture, and the translation from colonised culture to coloniser. The latter is readily understood from critical reflection on historical ethnographic museums and collections. Today we understand that so much of our interpretation of other cultures was through the prism of our own established ways of seeing. We readily reflect on how knowledge of other people was often used to support an ideological bias, including the idea of a European evolutionary, racial superiority. Thomas invites us to understand this process of meaning-making symmetrically. We may also be able to understand the appropriation by the colonised through discourse of an object's meaning as an act of resistance. Power may be asymmetrical but the role of discourse in forms of complicity and resistance is at the heart of its operations. So, too, the potential for creativity, for art practice, which, as storytelling, lies at the heart of the operations of power as both complicity and resistance.

The point in bringing in historical anthropology here is to demonstrate the operation of power and resistance as Foucault describes it. Resistance may not be recognised from the outside, misunderstood as acts of complicity or as something else, because it doesn't conform to our predefined notions of resistance.

'We never desire against our interests'

As the subject of this book is art and the artworld in this historical moment, I am interested in where and how we have appropriated neoliberalism and where this has, in the words of Nicholas Thomas, *entangled us in wider political and economic relations that are not easily shrugged off.* I am interested in where and how economic and political neoliberal values have been overlaid on our local 'native' values so that we are now subject to 'foreign rule' (to use an admittedly hyperbolic and inaccurate metaphor).

I have described instances of our willing complicity as artists in this process: where the artworld is a paragon of neoliberalism and where neoliberal structural changes have altered the structures of the artworld in ways that we have accepted as normal. Chin-tao Wu's analysis details how far these changes had already taken place by the early 2000s. The decades from the 1980s saw an increasing impact of the corporate sector on the artworld, but it is also worth remembering that it is no new phenomenon. At various moments throughout the twentieth century the very wealthy have had undue influence on democratic cultural institutions and art, as demonstrated in Donna Haraway's analysis of the origins of the American Museum of Natural History in the 1930s,[32] and infamously during the 1950s the US government made diplomatic use of abstract expressionism as an instrument of the Cold War.[33] What may be new, as evident with the rise of neoliberalism within the artworld, is a culture of corporatism, where we, the practitioners, readily accept commercial imperatives as 'reality'; we readily instrumentalise and measure ourselves in the service of state, commercial and corporate goals. To quote Gilles Deleuze in an interview with Foucault:

> it is clear who exploits, who profits, and who governs, but power nevertheless remains something more diffuse. I would venture the following hypothesis: the thrust of Marxism was to define the problem essentially in terms of interests (power is held by a ruling class defined by its interests). The question immediately arises: how is it that people whose interests are not being served can strictly support the existing power structure by demanding a piece of the action? Perhaps this is because in terms of *investments*, whether economic or unconscious, interest is not the final answer; there are investments of desire that function in a more profound and diffuse manner than our interests dictate. But of course, we never desire against our interests, because interest always follows and finds itself where desire has placed it. We cannot shut out the scream of Reich: the masses were not deceived; at a particular time, they actually wanted a fascist regime![34]

Perhaps, at this time, we actually desire a system that focuses the attention of our 'resistance' on imagined power structures, as if power operates as a binary, so that we may blithely replicate power relations and disavow responsibility and freedom. Clearly there is something in it for us or we would be doing, desiring, knowing and creating otherwise.

Neoliberal desire

Where neoliberal homilies intersect with artworld desire, our 'interests', can be seen variously in the idea that anything can be bought and sold with the right mechanism; that price reflects value; the higher the price, the higher the value of an object or service; that markets ultimately benefit all, just as a rising tide carries all boats. There is nothing that the market cannot provide; there is no public good or artistic product that should not or cannot, by its nature, be part of a market. Everything of value can be sold; things that cannot be sold therefore have no value. Only the market can establish value. Everyone wants to be rich. Wealth is an indicator of intelligence or ability. Price is an indicator of value. Competition is the mechanism of evolution. Competitive mechanisms create excellence. Tools that illuminate relative worth such as league tables (for example, the Artfacts website and the German business magazine *Capital*'s 'Art Compass') are preferable to mechanisms that foster absolute standards or intrinsic value, such as philosophical treatises or manifestos. Relative values are a safer measure than intrinsic values. Everything (of value) is measurable or it has no value.

These neoliberal axioms, many of which are now common within the artworld, are new beliefs and distinct from the beliefs held by previous generations of artists and others in the artworld. There are many historical, discursive and structural reasons that might account for this. Some have been discussed in a previous chapter and others will be discussed in the next chapter, but here I wish to emphasise how much we, as artists and others, now reflect neoliberalism within our very beliefs, hopes and professional dreams and that this happens freely, willingly, without coercion.

Thatcher asserted that *There Is No Alternative* to free market, globalised capitalism;[35] many other political leaders have attempted to convince the citizenry that there is no alternative. The totalitarian regimes of the twentieth century used coercion and fear to enforce the idea that there really was no alternative (and then they ended). There is no real comparison between the current system of enforcing 'no alternative' to deregulated free-market capitalism and the practices of coercive totalitarian regimes, but it is worth remembering that Sartre's Existentialism, conceived during Nazi occupation and the Vichy government in France, posited that there are always alternatives even under the most overtly oppressive of regimes. There is an intrinsic relationship between the individual and societies – mechanisms and the individuals that comprise them – enacting and embodying values and prejudices that are meant to be for the good of society or for the good of the individual as sanctioned by the nation state. It is we who believe there is no alternative and act as if this were true when no alternatives are presented. When beliefs are held as incontestable and popular, they are particularly difficult to analyse or to refute.

Within the artworld, norms are promulgated by other artists, theorists and curators; in other words, peers. If power operates through each of us individually – through our hopes, dreams, stories, relations – it can be extremely difficult to read the flow of discourse because we are part of its flow. Like any group in society, the artworld also has great normalising pressures on its actors. Like other parts of society, neoliberal values are now woven into the stories of those who claim to promote values other than neoliberalism or the market. Though few in the artworld even use the term neoliberalism to describe the set of values, many happily champion those values, assuming them to be commonsense, normal, even modern and of-the-moment. Yet they have only recently been internalised. Some of these values and norms have been absorbed by politicised, radical or socially engaged artists. This will be described in the next chapter.

Conclusion

The binary model, and the politics and art of negation, though rich and productive historically, must be understood as no longer helpful. It is an act of nostalgia to hang on to a past binary model and to continue to work within the artistic tropes that were established within that model. We are each of us constitutive of the various worlds in which we operate and a politics of engagement must start from that understanding. Foucault theorises an intimate relationship with power, embodied through the very desires, stories and knowledge that make up our identity and purpose. We are always both willing agents and potential resisters and it is through discourse – the stories we seek, promulgate, embody – that this occurs.

The binary, because it cannot escape its defining ground, replicates the centrality or dominance of that aspect of power defined through opposition. Rather than understanding power in terms of us and them, Foucault's notion of 'transmitting' power through the stories we seek out and pass on, and how we locate each other within available repertoires of human conduct and define patterns of social interaction, is not only a more accurate model but is more generative of the resistant, disruptive potential of art. This is the conclusion of this book. The conclusion of this chapter is that each of us is constitutive of power, free and responsible. We choose whether to believe in or act in accordance with neoliberal norms. We choose whether to replicate the self-evident truths promulgated within neoliberalism and whether we look at and understand the mechanisms of power at play within the artworld. This is not about whether, as individual artists, we choose to sell our work through dealers, or take commissions from the state, or find novel ways of funding our art practice – or traditional ways such as having a job. This is about the gamut of our actions and beliefs that inform our practice and our values, which ultimately – collectively – make up the artworld. The artworld currently operates as an embodiment of neoliberalism. Here I am making the case for a nuanced understanding of power, given that we are fundamentally part of its processes, and that we must recognise it is we, collectively, who have chosen a neoliberal artworld – unless we choose something else.

CHAPTER 4

The Art–Life Dichotomy

Summary

This chapter explores an artworld binary that has riven the realm of art from the realm of life. The binary is based on the legacy of a twentieth-century debate that is assumed to have longer historical roots. In this chapter, Allan Kaprow's art and writing becomes emblematic of the 'lifelike art' position, and that of philosopher Clement Greenberg is emblematic of the 'artlike art' position. There is far more complexity to the debate but, as in the previous chapter, my aim is not for accurate historiography but to explore the detrimental legacy of this debate and the assumptions about good art that stem from it, including ideas around autonomy. I argue that this binary – actually a simplistic misreading of Kant – has created a legacy in which continuing assumptions about art linger into the twenty-first century: there is an ongoing injunction for practitioners who espouse a leftist or radical politics to make art in a particular way, namely in the tradition of lifelike art. Lifelike art includes relational, dialogic, participatory and community-orientated practices. It also includes 'dematerialized' art and new media or new technology. Lifelike art is assumed to carry, by its very nature, a revolutionary or democratic politics. Artlike art, on the other hand, is assumed to be apolitical, because it is perceived as removed from the social arena and intrinsically hierarchical because of the assumed distance from the social. Because of these assumptions, artists and curators fail to recognise radicalism and subversion when it happens in another register. We also tend to assume that lifelike art realises its political promise. This is not always the case. Art practitioners in the lifelike tradition, instead of embodying or enacting a subversive disruption, now value measurement, populism and efficacy, which are all neoliberal values and values notably absent within the artworld prior to the rise of neoliberalism.

◆ ◆ ◆ ◆

The dichotomy

The previous chapter described how the artworld continues to be enthralled with binary models. Not only are these models theoretically incoherent given that the artworld claims a theoretical basis in Foucault, Rancière, Mouffe and Laclau, but the binary model of power prevalent within the artworld reproduces discourses of authenticity and recuperation, which ultimately disempower and disavow most forms of resistance by creating sites of 'authentic' resistance and authentic modes of art. This chapter will look at another part of the binary model prevalent within the artworld, which has led not only to its own theoretical cul-de-sac, but inadvertently to the internalisation of neoliberal values. Here I focus on assumptions found in the wider spectrum of the non-market-orientated artworld, that which is less institutionally and commercially supported, in addition to the monied, state- and corporate-sponsored biennial sector.

There are a number of ways in which the focus on established artworld binaries has created the conditions for neoliberal mechanisms and assumptions to become norms within the artworld. Before I describe these, I will first say that I am not advocating that the proper position for artists is to resist 'exogenous' incursions such as market forces or neoliberal values. My argument is not to advocate a politically or aesthetically homogeneous artworld. It is an argument for genuine diversity. What I am saying is that there are many practitioners who claim that art should be about things other than, or in addition to, serving the market, and some practitioners claim specifically to want to resist oppressive, exploitative capitalist or neoliberal values. For those who share these values, therefore, my argument is that we inspect artworld assumptions and consider whether or not current artworld norms help practitioners to realise these goals of resistance and alterity. We must examine artworld assumptions and understand where they intersect with neoliberal mechanisms, as these mechanisms act to reduce choice and genuine freedoms despite professing the opposite.

My concern here is art and the important role that art plays in society, as distinct from any other type of action. This importance will be described in detail in Part III. Here I assume art's importance and instead focus on artworld discourse. If art is defined by the artworld, as argued in Part I, by definition art will be a specific set of media, processes, types of display, etc. As described by Danto, art is defined through a set of writing, narratives, discourse. If an artist is concerned to make art, they will conform to artworld discourse and its prescriptions. If, on the other hand, a person is concerned with *doing good things in the world*, their focus will lie elsewhere, with no regard to artworld norms and discourse. A person primarily concerned with doing good things in the world will ignore the artworld prescriptions on process, media, display as they are irrelevant to the goal of doing good in the world. Instead they might focus on doing good things in the world through, for example, education, activism or engineering. But an artist must adhere to artworld prescriptions as it is the artworld that legitimates practice; the artworld confers the status of art on to an object, process, display. An artist who is interested in the political or social must concede the normative operations of the artworld and either make and display art in accordance with them or try to alter artworld discourse. I am both investigating discourse as it operates to normalise a binary around good art and trying to alter it.

The binary explored here is characterised as art–life. Understood by the artworld to be the legacy of Kantian philosophy, it continues to have currency. According to Robert Yanal, it is not Kant who creates a division between art and life but this interpretation is a twentieth-century reductive misreading of his philosophy by Clive Bell, which has been reproduced ever since.[1] Famous for their writing in the twentieth century in the art–life binary tradition are artist Allan Kaprow, who wrote from the late 1950s until the 1980s espousing lifelike art, and philosopher Clement Greenberg, who is characterised as espousing artlike art and a reductive version of 'art for art's sake'. The idea of art for art's sake became associated with a right-wing and market-orientated art in the twentieth century. In the nineteenth century, it had its own leftist political overtones. In contrast to the Saint-Simonists who were overtly interested in instrumentalising art for social ends, art for art's sake was understood to be another strategy 'in opposition to the bourgeois, profit-orientated society of the July monarchy', as Bätschmann argues.[2] Like the assumptions around lifelike and artlike art, the idea of art for art's sake is distorted and simplified by many artists and theorists working today, because we have uncritically accepted a binary model as part of our inheritance; Greenberg casts a long shadow. Historical truths are inherently contestable but history is always more complex than a binary model describes. This chapter sets out to undermine the assumptions within the art–life binary – and the histories presented here will help to undermine the assumed truths within that binary.

In 'The Real Experiment' (1983) Kaprow defines the terms artlike and lifelike that I will use in this chapter and he claims a deeper history for the art–life binary, embedding it even further within our history by claiming that the split goes back to ancient Rome:

> Western art actually has two avant-garde histories, one of artlike art and the other of lifelike art. They've been lumped together as parts of a succession of movements fervently committed to innovation, but they represent fundamentally contrasting philosophies of reality.
>
> Simplistically put, artlike art holds that art is separate from life and everything else, whereas lifelike art holds that art is connected to life and everything else. In other words, there is art at the service of art and art at the service of life.[3]

Many champions of the tradition of lifelike art, including Lucy Lippard, perceive their end of the artistic spectrum as political, or at least politicised, specifically because it is involved with the social.[4] By contrast, a Greenbergian position is understood as depoliticised or 'right wing' within the artworld specifically because it disavows the importance of the social. It came to be understood as market-serving since the market appears to be the default position for an 'apolitical' or 'asocial' stance, being suitably and compatibly rarefied. This is not an inevitable reading: T. J. Clark, with his long-standing commitment to Marxist politics, revisited the type of art that Greenberg favours, arguing that it was in fact a negotiation with socialism.[5] Nevertheless, Greenberg's position on art *is* hierarchical and elitist, famously dismissing as 'kitsch' the types of art he doesn't favour.[6]

Competing notions of autonomy

For Greenberg, it was above all aesthetic judgement, by which he meant judgements of taste, and the distinctive kind of experience he associated with such judgements, that underwrote the value of art as art. The project Greenberg set for Modernist painting, for example, was an investigation into the essential nature of painting, working towards what was 'unique and irreducible' to the medium, that is 'flatness and the delimitation of flatness', as Diarmuid Costello describes.[7] For Greenberg, therefore, the goal of art lies in its transcendence, art's autonomy from the social realm:

> Art and the history of art can be approached and discussed illuminatingly all by themselves, as though taking place in an area of experience that's autonomous, a place that doesn't have to be connected with any other area of experience in order to have sense made of it. What I've just said is the most radical expression I can think of what's called vulgarly 'formalism' ... asking art to serve a moral, or any other end except aesthetic quality, is to make an illegitimate demand on art.[8]

The type of art that refers to art-specific qualities or values only, such as colour and form, and with little or no reference to narratives or the social or political realm is known as formalism. Understood as the acme of a teleological tale of art-historical progress, it was a centrally important idea for Alfred Barr, first Director of the Museum of Modern Art, and philosophers Clive Bell and Clement Greenberg. To them, Cubism or Abstract Expressionism, being types of art primarily concerned with qualities within art itself, were the epitome of Modernism, indeed the epitome of *man's* achievement. They are 'autonomous' art forms, free from connection to the social realm and therefore superior to other forms of art practice.[9] In this way, the idea of autonomy came to be equated with Modernism by the artworld. Once Modernism was critiqued and surpassed by postmodernism in the 1980s and 1990s, autonomy took on a dubious flavour. However, in addition to this specific meaning, autonomy has other meanings in a Marxist tradition and in its usage by Kant.

In common usage, the idea of autonomy is the right to self-government or a sense of independence from external pressures or influence. One strand within the Marxist idea of autonomy is the specific relation of the artist to their production, where art is understood as an act of expression of the authentic self in defiance of alienating conditions. This is a position articulated by philosopher Adolfo Sánchez Vázquez. Describing the process of alienation by which the autonomy of art production is undermined, he writes:

> In capitalist society, a work of art is 'productive' when it is market-orientated, when it submits itself to the exigencies of the market, the fluctuations of supply and demand. And since there is no objective measure by which to determine the value of his particular merchandise, the artist is subject to the tastes, preferences, ideas, and aesthetic notions of those who influence the market. Inasmuch as he produces works of art destined for a market that absorbs them, the artist cannot fail to heed the exigencies of this market: they often affect the content as well as the form of a work of art thus placing limitations on the artist ... A form of alienation is thus produced, denaturalising the essence of artistic work.[10]

Within this Marxist tradition, the external, alienating conditions that obstruct autonomous artistic production are understood as the market. Once again, we can see exemplified in this piece the assumptions within the Marxist binary model of authenticity and inauthenticity, where autonomy is more or less the equivalent of authenticity.

For Kant, the autonomy of the will is deducible from the unconditional command of the conscience or reason. In other words, the autonomous self is the rational free self, as distinct from the idea of a self ruled by the sensorium, for example by pleasure or pain. Kant's idea of autonomy has an emphasis on reason as freedom, as distinct from feelings, the senses or the passions, but it doesn't simply echo David Hume's idea of a self that is 'slave' to its passions in a dialectic with reason. Instead, a rational will must be regarded as autonomous or free as it creates the laws that bind it. Further, these acts of autonomy will always be, by definition, moral acts. The incomparable dignity of human beings derives from the fact that we are:

> free with respect to all laws of nature, obeying only those rules which he himself gives and in accordance with which his maxims can belong to a giving of universal law (to which at the same time he subjects himself).[11]

The legacy of the myriad and conflicting usages of the word autonomy for the artworld has created a set of ideas that are muddled and yet inflexible because they carry binary overtones of good–bad, inside–outside. Curator Jan Verwoert's essay for *Curating and the Educational Turn* (2010) exemplifies this multiple history and its legacy for the artworld. He both rejects and embraces autonomy:

> To invoke the attunement to the inherent potentials of a creative process as a means of realising relative autonomy is, admittedly, a modernist move, but I think that such a move is needed now in defiance of the demands to industrialise communication. But, this defiance would have to be performed in a new, contemporary mode. In their more mindless moments, many classical modernists interpreted autonomy as a fantasy of removing oneself to untouchable places. That their interpretation was escapist doesn't imply that the desire for autonomy is necessarily so. The point now is to relocate this desire to a touchable place. This means rethinking autonomy within the horizon of precisely those cultural practices that much classical modernist thought relegated to the

sphere of heteronomy – the practices of diplomatic brokering necessitated by mutual social dependencies.[12]

A good–bad binary around the idea of autonomy was established for the artworld by the mid-twentieth century so that some types of practice and concepts lie *ipso facto* on one side and others lie on the other.

Modernity and art

When considering twentieth-century art, artists tend to be encouraged to look to the social history, and theories from the mid-twentieth century built on the nineteenth-century foundations of Hegel and Marx (as well as Freud). This is too narrow a focus. Perhaps it is by focusing on so narrow and somewhat overdetermined a piece of history that we are led to the more futile debates and dichotomies. Art historian Oskar Bätschmann describes the art of a modern era where modernity begins in the eighteenth century and with the Enlightenment, as opposed to the end of the nineteenth century.[13] He describes a history of the debates around art practice, commerce and autonomy that complicates any simple dichotomy as a historically supported truism that both Greenberg and Kaprow suppose.[14] There has never been a hallowed past when disinterested artistic values reigned in the artworld. Nor has there been entirely a relationship of bad faith. Greenberg wrote of an 'umbilical cord of gold' and that 'the avant-garde remained attached to bourgeois society precisely because it needed its money'.[15] This is too simplistic. There is a long history to the tension between artists, audiences and systems of resources (and the systems of thought that yield them), and individual artists have negotiated these tensions differently throughout history.[16]

Art–life: a theoretical cul-de-sac

There is a widely held assumption within the artworld, based on the legacy of the Greenberg–Kaprow dichotomy, that lifelike art is inherently more distant from market mechanisms and commercialism than artlike art. There is also the assumption that lifelike art is best placed to critique commodification, the market, capitalism and neoliberalism. This assumption is shared by Nicolas Bourriaud, Claire Bishop, Grant Kester, Gregory Sholette, Suzanne Lacy and most others working in the lifelike art tradition. Bishop observes that 'as an artistic medium ... participation [one form of lifelike art] is arguably no more intrinsically political or oppositional than any other'; nevertheless, her edited collection of essays and artworks, *Participation* (2006), serves to fuel the binary and its assumptions of good–bad, political–apolitical by reiterating the debate on traditional binary lines.[17]

The binary is not as striking today as it was in the twentieth century, in that artlike art is more rarely produced, but it is evident that the assumptions within the lifelike tradition continue, particularly around money and the purpose of art, and the correct media for its ambitions. One of the many consequences that stem from the binary is that artists who make lifelike art are more inclined to obfuscate their relationship to commerce, as biennial artists tend to do; those in the wider lifelike art part of the artworld tend to reject outright commerce, commodification and capitalist values as an integral part of their practice. This overtly political or socially engaged part of the artworld tends to be found in the UK in universities, art colleges and the education departments of museums and, when externally supported and not self-funded, it is in the form of public subsidy via various smaller arts organisations, agencies and higher education funding bodies. Here we find those artists who wish to operate in a way that resists the market for ethical or political reasons. Many are the inheritors of a 1960s and 1970s Conceptual Art perspective and its direct challenge to commodification, the market and capitalism. The more overtly political also cite the Situationist International as artistic predecessors. With this legacy comes the unexamined assumption that 'dematerialised' art is inherently uncommodifiable. Happenings, events, live art, and the ephemera of conceptual art that occurred in the 1960s and 1970s, as well as the site-specific interventions, activist art and pedagogical art in the 1990s and 2000 were/are supposed to be uncommodifiable. Lippard writes:

> Hopes that 'conceptual art' would be able to avoid the general commercialisation, the destructively 'progressive' approach of modernism were for the most part unfounded. It seemed in 1969 … that no one, not even a public greedy for novelty, would actually pay money, or much of it, for a Xerox sheet referring to an event past or never directly perceived, a group of photographs documenting an ephemeral situation or condition, a project for work never to be completed, words spoken but not recorded; it seemed that these artists would therefore be forcibly freed from the tyranny of a commodity status and market-orientation.[18]

The advent of the knowledge economy, described in Part I, rang the death knell for any such utopian tactic. Nevertheless, art practices using dematerialised forms or media such as the internet are still understood as inherently politicised, and the media and practices imagined to be outside the market are perceived as more ethical, more political, more disruptive.[19] In this way, for example, painting can never be understood as a potent medium in the lifelike tradition, whereas photography is, despite the fact that most contemporary photography replicates the problematics of painting as critiqued within the lifelike tradition.[20]

Framed and delimited by past debates, assumptions continue about politicised or ethical practices. The legacy of Kaprow is to prescribe the appropriate media and methodology, processes or display for lifelike or socially engaged practices. By and large, art that questions market norms or norms that maintain the status quo continues to be made using a limited range of media, namely the dematerialised or new media. There is also a corresponding limitation to the range of processes: relational, dialogic, multiple-authored or community-located being the primary modes legitimated for a lifelike practice. In terms of display, art that questions market or neoliberal norms is almost invariably 'documentary' or 'ethnographic' (based on mistaken assumptions about anthropological process). Those acts of resistance that use any of the other forms of art-making or display are misrecognised as such. By conforming to orthodoxies about appropriate media or process or display, we not only limit our own choices about how to make art but we also limit our potential to comprehend a world full of active resistance, misreading those actions or artworks through our own artworld clichés and norms. Johanna Drucker's *Sweet Dreams: Contemporary Art and Complicity* at least starts to make a case for the resistive potential of other types of practice.[21]

When understanding these artworld normative operations from a Foucauldian perspective, as the previous chapter describes, it is clear that we are subject to, and subject each other to, normative disciplines, locating each other within available repertoires of human conduct and defining patterns of social interaction. The very idea of a *correct* way of making resistant art is clearly part of this disciplining process, denying the potential for acts of resistance by simply disavowing action not recognised within the prescriptions of the normative model. Instead of being aware of this process of disciplining artworld knowledge, expelling or ignoring deviation, such debate becomes a way of policing the boundary of 'good' art in these binary terms, as the debate between Grant Kester and Claire Bishop aired in *Artforum* shows. On one side of the binary, good art *refuses* artworld norms as the artworld is too rarefied to be socially effective, while on the other side of the binary, good art *conforms* to artworld norms because having artworld norms helps to determine good art.[22] Because this desire to value a lifelike art practice in terms of aesthetics is understood as conforming to the dubious hierarchies of Greenberg's artlike art, it is incendiary. Tempers on both sides fray and intentions are perhaps wilfully misunderstood. Rather than continuing to engage in the debates that bolster and maintain the binary, the debate should be seen as, at best, a diversion and, at worst, lending itself to the inadvertent reproduction of neoliberal techniques of power.

Instead of examining artworld power and its operations, our own agency and ourselves as part of the techniques of power, we tend to rest on methodological tropes that 'guarantee' an ethical or political reading. The legacy of this debate has meant that we have become less reflexive about the values and mechanisms that actually inform our work. The absence of a conscious awareness of, and continued reflection on, these values has also created the situation where even those artists on the left have instrumentalised ourselves in the service of neoliberal goals, as will be described.

Artlike art and judgement, lifelike art and measurement

The idea of a critical aesthetic judgement has informed art appreciation and art practice consciously and overtly at least since Immanuel Kant's *Critique of Judgement* in 1790. Art was judged for its aesthetic worth and, in various periods throughout art history, artists and others in the artworld codified these aesthetic rules, which subsequent generations rebelled against, thus creating new rules, tastes and orthodoxies. In the mid-twentieth century, this process of art-historical negation was given greater potency with the art–life rift. Aesthetic judgement might be applied to artlike art, because it is apolitical and hierarchical, but lifelike art brooked no such inherently problematic mechanism of distinction. For the lifelike artists, aesthetic judgement is inherently elitist and hierarchical. Clement Greenberg played a part in fuelling this perception.

With postmodernism, the lifelike tradition critiqued Modernism and artlike art. We distanced ourselves from its tropes, subverting values such as truth, beauty and originality because they served to depoliticise art, deny its social efficacy, or they created false hierarchies, maintaining Eurocentric, gender-specific normalising discourse (genius as the province of white men; beauty the province of white women; truth the product of the European Enlightenment). We said that art is anything we say it is and everybody is an artist, but, as described in Part I, this turned out to be not entirely true. Whereas the artlike tradition openly embraced aesthetic judgement and its translation into monetary value and class distinction, the lifelike tradition operates in bad faith. There is a false openness in lifelike art practice and a false distance from commerce because, despite the fact that the lifelike tradition holds the values of anti-hierarchy, inclusivity and anti-commodification, in reality it operates to police its boundaries and create value just as the artlike art tradition does. This is necessarily the case as described in the Institutional definition of art.

The legacy of lifelike art is that we have sidestepped the issue of judgement and value and, as Benjamin Buchloh has observed, instead we have allowed the market to decide.[23] From the start of the Enlightenment with the end of the *Ancien Régime*, the idea of aesthetic judgement – the question of who can judge and on what grounds – was contested, but with the rise of neoliberalism, the idea of judgement was replaced by the idea of measurement.[24]

Today it is hard to imagine the value of an artwork or art practice that has neither a commodity value nor social enterprise goal attached. Artists and curators have internalised these values and we now willingly measure the impact of our own work. There is an absence of discourse articulating art's unique value, because we have distanced ourselves from those values articulated within the artlike tradition (truth, beauty, originality). This has created the space for an unwitting internalisation of neoliberal mechanisms and values for artists working in the lifelike tradition. The idea of efficacy, measuring whether an artwork or exhibition achieved its goal, has been taken up especially by activist, community-orientated, dialogic and pedagogical art practitioners.

With the rise of neoliberalism, measurement and targets have become normal, even desirable, within the lifelike tradition. Andrew Brighton, writing on the artworld at the time of New Labour, described its targets and measurement-driven culture and its impact on the arts as Stalinist, assuming that New Labour had its ideological roots in communism.[25] In fact, the type of measurement employed by New Labour was neoliberal, both a tool of business and a technology of government as described by Foucault. Measurement is a technology of government and it has been a mechanism of the state in novel ways since the New Labour government in 1997, as Neil Barnett, lecturer in public policy, describes:

> governmentality works through the 'conduct of conduct' and ... control is exercised through the management of freedom, or self-regulation. ... In all cases the emphasis is upon 'the responsibilisation of the self' and of instilling reflexive self-control ... These 'technologies of the self' allow for the connection between the 'micro politics' of everyday behaviour and broad political rationalities.[26]

It is through measuring ourselves that we operate on ourselves on behalf of the government. Some parts of the artworld, namely the commercial and artlike part of the artworld, have been measuring themselves for decades. Measuring art in terms of price, and creating league tables on this basis, German business journal *Capital* has published since 1970 an annual league table, 'Art Compass', valuing artists hierarchically in monetary terms. A later instantiation of an artworld-embraced hierarchy is the website Artfacts.net, which is supposedly a more nuanced and truer picture of artworld hierarchies of importance, as it is econometric, based on an algorithm that includes exhibition attention as well as price. Hierarchies and measurement are both a hallmark of traditional right-wing politics and a feature of neoliberal technologies of power. They instantiate and validate a world view in which some are valued highly while others have little or no value.[27]

Until postmodernism crushed the last vestiges of the Romantic hero-artist myth, avant-garde artists, working before their time and alone, could take comfort in the idea that it would be future generations that would one day catch up and that present invisibility simply proved that their work was indeed anti-bourgeois, difficult and therefore at the cutting edge and important. Contemporary artists have no such comforting discourse. Not only has postmodernism rendered ridiculous the myths of Romanticism but neoliberalism has rendered the idea of difficulty as elitist.

Artists in the lifelike tradition have found other ways to negotiate value and visibility. With the rise of neoliberalism, and in the absence of any artworld values to counter or complement the artlike tradition, the left-end of the political spectrum began also to measure art in order to ascertain worth. Politicised practitioners working assiduously outside market values suddenly want to measure their work in terms of social impact or efficacy.

Impact may include numbers of audience, types of participants, newspaper and magazine column inches or hits on websites. For those in the lifelike tradition, value is not in econometric or monetary terms, but in terms of social good or efficacy. Just as the state started to value art as a panacea for social ills ranging from social exclusion to 'poverty of aspiration' to threat from terrorism, socially engaged and radical artists also started to value art in terms of efficacy and measure it in terms of impact.

Good art has a mass audience and an observable, measurable impact. This new view of art's value is one actively supported by the Arts Council of England, requiring that practitioners measure art in these terms in order to gain funding. Most recently, practitioners have begun to value their art in these terms even when working on projects with no funding.

This requirement has created the question of evidence. If art does ameliorate social ills, and artists and organisations receive funding on this basis, then evidence must be provided to support the claim. In the case of fine art, the idea of evidence is so fraught that critics of New Labour's arts policy such as Munira Mirza and Sara Selwood had an open goal: a range of problematically soft, even false, statistical evidence was provided by artists and arts institutions to substantiate claims on the public purse.[28]

By unthinkingly replicating the norms and assumptions within the lifelike art legacy, we have allowed ourselves to become instruments of neoliberal power. We measure ourselves and value art only insofar as it is valuable within neoliberal mechanisms of 'self-responsibilisation', as Barnett describes. Market-orientated art is no longer the only instantiation of neoliberalism in the artworld. Those who have wanted art to have some kind of social role are now fundamentally part of a neoliberal state's mechanisms.

Populism and democracy

The idea of populism, like the idea of judgement, has been debated throughout the modern era once art's previously assured place in society ended, along with aristocratic and church patronage. Artists such as Jacques-Louis David (1748–1825), who made self-consciously popular artworks, appealed to the public as the best arbiter of greatness in art.[29] Echoed two hundred years later in Jeff Koon's statements about making art 'almost like television', Koons is quoted as saying that he always tries 'at least to get the mass of people in the door'.[30] The populist argument is countered by James Barry (1741–1806), one of the six founding members of the Royal Academy and a contemporary of Jacques-Louis David. Barry argued to the contrary, that populism was antithetical to a great artistic practice. Accusing patrons of ruining artistic talent, and artists of yielding to the corruption of commercial interests, Barry contrasted the corrupted artists with the morality of the 'real artist', who stood firmly against 'fraud and wrong', with no thought of personal gain, doing his 'duty to God and his country regardless of whether he ultimately proved to be a martyr or a conqueror'.[31] This is not to say, however, that throughout the modern era there was a continuity to the debate about populism. Debate has always been in response to specific historical, political and economic circumstances. The references to duty, God and country in the James Barry quote underline the historical context of his position.

Artworld debates about populism and value have specific nuances within neoliberalism. One of the great unacknowledged successes of neoliberalism has been the acceptance of the idea, even within the artworld, that if something has only a small audience it must be too difficult and therefore elitist: it has failed in its duty of access to attract the widest possible audience. No longer is it possible to want to stage an exhibition that is so experimental or so radically different from what is already successful that it might be difficult to find an audience in any great number. With a market model, genuine novelty as new starting points for art cannot exist. As described in Part I, monoculturalism through the endless permutation of an established matrix is the inevitable endpoint of a highly organised market. The market generalises in order to kill off other potential markets and puts in place various forms of cooperation with the aim of sharing uncertainties; goods and processes tend to become standardised.[32] Within neoliberal norms, it might seem obvious that state- and corporate-sponsored art and exhibitions require a level of popularity to justify funding, but populism is an invidious concept. The market becomes sole or primary arbiter of value, be it the elite market where value is based on price or the mass market where value is derived from volume. By valuing populism, a discourse is created that relegates as secondary or irrelevant those values that are in addition to, or outside, the market: singular or small acts that may have been valued in aesthetic or radical terms become useless, failures or irrelevant within discourses of populism. Even the lifelike and radical parts of the artworld have internalised this neoliberal value, privileging the world stage and mass audiences as the only way to validate or value art. Anything smaller, less visible, is failure irrespective of the quality of the artwork in the first place.

Numbers and politics

Here I need to make a distinction between art and activism or politics. Whereas mass audiences and populism are a new and neoliberal value within the artworld, numbers have always been important for activists. Measurement of impact, efficacy and the drive to gain support from ever larger sectors of the community is how democratic action works. It is the politics of multitude expressed by Paolo Virno, Antonio Negri and Michael Hardt.[33] These are important considerations in the political realm, whether the politics is mainstream – in the form of political parties, campaigning or trades unions – or whether it is the politics of direct action. Art, however, is not an action of the multitude.

The reason for distinguishing between art and politics is because, in the absence of endogenous artworld-specific values, another legacy of the lifelike tradition is the elision of lifelike art with politics, which has served to undermine the unique importance and value of both activist practice and art practice. In mistaking one for the other, not only has the artworld inadvertently internalised the neoliberal values of measurement and populism, but we have missed what is important and valuable about art. In order to validate a socially engaged, political or lifelike art practice, the values of politics have been overlaid on art practice. Because of the assumptions within the art–life binary, that part of the artworld that actively resists the market has allowed efficacy, populism and other forms of measurement to become ways of valuing art practice. These ideas, appropriate to the world of politics and perhaps education, when translated to the artworld, become instances of internalised neoliberal values. Art practice is not education or activism, nor any other praxis or discipline. Nor should it emulate those praxes for which efficacy or populism may be appropriate values.

Conclusion

The idea of aesthetic judgement is rightly dismissed within the lifelike art tradition, but the lack of endogenous values within the artworld has resulted in obscured hierarchical structures built on the absence of any open criteria for valuing art, as Velthuis observed.[34] We have created a covertly hierarchical system even within the lifelike art part of the artworld, while claiming to despise hierarchy and exclusion. This is because, on the one hand, the artworld by definition polices the boundary of art. On the other, this process of valuing and exclusion is based on veiled criteria. The value of art is not articulated in its own terms, even by practitioners. Instead, mechanisms based on networks of power within the artworld (described by Gielen and Velthuis) determine a value that is elitist because it is esoteric and opaque. Neglecting to assert our endogenous values, relying solely on recognisable and stereotypical 'radical' processes, forms and methods – including those that mimic education and activism – neoliberal values and goals have been internalised by the artworld with counterproductive outcomes for the lifelike tradition. Art urgently needs a discourse of validation – of value – that is endogenous, because without one we are unable to counter prevailing myths and hegemonic forces, even if that is our desire. If we cannot articulate the role and value of art for society, that value will be determined by the operations of power, the market and neoliberalism.

Part III
A Celebration of Art Practice

I have argued that the legacy of the twentieth-century debates described in Part II has undermined the potential for understanding a radical or dissenting art practice. Both the binary model of power that is traditionally perceived within the artworld and the assumptions within the lifelike art tradition have, in the twenty-first century, served only to replicate the values and mechanisms of neoliberalism, and realise neither social nor artistic goals. In answer, Part III offers two things for those artists interested in radical practice and alterity. It offers another way of understanding art practice, this from a practitioner's point of view, in order to value what we do as artists and our role in society. Chapter 5 proposes the idea that we understand art as a knowledge-forming discipline akin to any other type of knowledge-forming discipline. This is proposed strategically, in order to articulate a definition and a value for art that refuses neoliberal norms and values. It is a way of articulating endogenous values without resorting to the problematic and thoroughly critiqued tropes within Modernism. Not only does understanding art as a discipline help to create alliances with other disciplines that similarly work with a set of values that are distinct from market values, but by being open about our operations we actually serve our core disciplinary values of freedom and, to a lesser extent, equality rather than the opposite. Chapter 6 reiterates the arguments presented here and celebrates what art actually does in society, as distinct from activism, education or any other type of praxis or discipline. Drawing on Hannah Arendt, the final chapter articulates a social and political value of art as both an instantiation of plurality and an action in the social realm, thereby defining it.

CHAPTER 5

The Disciplinarity of Art Practice

Summary

This chapter is a proposal for a new discourse through which to value art. There is a pressing need to redefine the value of art: with the rise of neoliberalism, art's value has been wholly subsumed within the values and mechanisms of neoliberalism. The artworld has lost a way of articulating the value of what we do and art is now understood either directly in market terms, or indirectly in other neoliberal terms, as a measurable instrument for the amelioration of social ills as defined or at least sanctioned by government. This chapter offers a way of understanding the value of art that is novel and yet also comes out of art's history. In the past, art has been understood as a knowledge-forming discipline. Yet while art has this history it is barely understood in these terms today, except where it is subsumed and denatured by academic institutions as part of the race to acquire qualifications. My proposal is that we understand art practice as part of a knowledge-forming discipline in a way that has its analogue in the processes, mechanisms and contributions of other knowledge-forming disciplines. By understanding art in this way, we may assert our own values against the increasing normalisation of neoliberal values, just as other disciplines such as medicine, anthropology or philosophy have core values that negotiate other values within society at any given time. Strategically, core disciplinary values can be seen as a way of carving out values and spaces that are distinct from the market and neoliberal values. Understanding art practice as a knowledge-forming discipline helps us to articulate what is art and what is not art in a way that is open and honest, as well as describing what is good art in endogenous disciplinary terms instead of, as is now the case, through neoliberal and market values.

◆ ◆ ◆ ◆

Many books have been written and conferences convened that start from a market point of view about the value of art and conclude with the idea that narrow economics cannot supply the full value of the aesthetic experience.[1] The artworld has relinquished its role in supplying this value for a number of historical and ideological reasons, and previous chapters have described how the absence of an endogenous artworld value or role for art has unwittingly paved the way for the acceptance of market measurements and neoliberal mechanisms. Even in 1979, Jean-François Lyotard wrote ironically that 'in the absence of aesthetic criteria':

> it remains possible and useful to assess the value of works of art according to the profits they yield. Such realism accommodates all tendencies, just as capital accommodates all 'needs', providing that the tendencies and needs have purchasing power. As for taste, there is no need to be delicate when one speculates or entertains oneself.[2]

Artists who position themselves *contra-power* have ended up neatly fitting themselves within the neoliberal value system,[3] embodying and replicating those mechanisms of power. In the attempt to describe the value of an art that is not market-orientated, art practice has been mistaken for activism, for education, for journalism, and even for anthropology. This may be because these types of praxis or discipline have easily identified values that are specifically not market-led. But art too is something important and unique in society. It is to our detriment and the detriment of society as a whole when we confuse art with other types of activity. Equally, other types of activity are profoundly misunderstood or misvalued when they are understood as art.

This chapter uses the idea of disciplinarity in order to articulate a meaning and value for art. For an artist working within the lifelike tradition, this is a bold move. Disciplinarity carries a number of right-wing overtones. In the first instance, it conjures Clement Greenberg and his pronouncements on artlike art; it flies in the face of assumptions made within the lifelike tradition that art is anything we say it is and everybody is an artist. I have already argued that the artworld actually operates in ways that sabotage these favoured homilies. Yet because we still perpetuate the myth of inclusivity and democracy, we operate in bad faith, obscuring the mechanisms and values operating at the heart of the artworld. In the process, we have created a closed elitist system that mitigates against meritocracy, the core artistic value of freedom and the lifelike art value of equality. The idea of disciplinarity also carries Foucauldian censorious overtones that chime well with the lifelike tradition of anti-discipline.[4] However, it is notable that Foucault meticulously argues for the specific methodology of genealogy in the place of history, spelling out clear disciplinary standards. This is with the proviso that we understand that:

> The intellectual's role is no longer to place himself 'somewhat ahead and to the side' in order to express the stifled truth of collectivity; rather, it is to struggle against the forms of power that transform him into its object and instrument

> in the sphere of 'knowledge', 'truth', 'consciousness' and 'discourse'. In this sense theory does not express, translate or serve practice: it is practice. But local and regional ... and not totalizing.[5]

Just as Foucault promotes genealogy as the appropriate mode of practice for his discipline once the nature of power is understood, this chapter promotes first that we understand art practice as a knowledge-forming discipline and, second, where our project lies within that discipline. Art practice (and in this chapter I emphasise art practice from a practitioner's point of view) must find a language of value that is endogenous (to use a term from anthropology). In this chapter I define art practice as a distinct discipline with its own mores, knowledge base, language, methodologies, blindspots, assumptions and, specifically, assumptions about what counts as knowledge. I argue that art practice is comparable with, and necessarily distinct from, any other (academic) discipline, be it philosophy, art history, archaeology or anthropology. This entails a discussion of what makes a discipline, recognising that what counts as knowledge is different in different disciplines and that these distinctions help to form discipline identity. I will also define art as a type of praxis, where praxis is understood as a form of conscious, willed action consequent of theoretical, philosophical or political commitment. Both academic disciplines and praxis disciplines, such as education and activism, share ways of self-legitimating and self-regulating. Here I overtly take up my artworld role in policing the boundary of art practice. I argue that not only is art different from other academic disciplines but it is a distinct praxis, different from activism, psychotherapy and education. By viewing art in this way, we will be better able to value the achievement of art, wrestling its achievements from neoliberal and other totalising, exogenous value systems.

What is a discipline?

The point of graduate education may be said to be, broadly, to create and reproduce the systems and values of the middle and ruling classes and, more narrowly, to inculcate in the individual student the values, biases, assumptions, ways of seeing and knowledges of the discipline area they have chosen to study. In the first years, students learn the lexicon and grammar specific to their subject area. They also learn methodologies, including interpretive skills (such as reading ECGs in medicine, reading spectrography in chemistry, reading paintings and sculpture in art practice and art history). Disciplinary practices are also learnt, such as sifting through archaeological detritus to differentiate between bones and other stuff, generating statistics, writing genealogies, using tools and mediums, phlebotomy. The final year of a degree brings the chance to display disciplinary credentials, to create 'masterpieces', to use the medieval idea of an artisanal work done at the end of an apprenticeship to demonstrate mastery. Exams and final exhibitions demonstrate how well a student has mastered the skills, knowledge sets, languages, norms and assumptions of a given discipline. These inform an individual's point of view, framing the experience of the world profoundly and potentially for the rest of their life, even if they later also learn about other discipline areas. In this sense, undergraduate education is formative both of class and of individual schema on to which subsequent adult experiences and knowledge are mapped.

The profound differences in individuals' worldview acquired through disciplinarity at tertiary level is rarely acknowledged. Instead, there is an assumption that knowledge and language are universal and immutable. Yet disciplines are in fact distinct, producing different assumptions and schema. They have edges that are policed. To highlight these differences I have used terms from outside the artworld: exogenous and endogenous. I employ these terms, found in anthropology, self-consciously to highlight the idea that differences between disciplines are either not seen as such or are overemphasised. I use these terms to evoke an artworld that is both as diverse and apparently coherent as those completely 'different' cultures that ethnographers attempt to comprehend.

It is possible to map the edge of a discipline, as what is acceptable knowledge or practice in one may be unacceptable or illegitimate in another. Jonas Salk's introduction to Latour and Woolgar's *Laboratory Life* (1979) is a case in point. *Laboratory Life* was a groundbreaking work of anthropology, exploring the social construction of a scientific fact through a fine-grained ethnography of one biology laboratory over time. Salk, a virologist, lead researcher of the polio vaccine and founder of the Salk Institute for Biological Research, wrote in his introduction that Latour's sociological research has insight. It may even be useful from his point of view *as a scientist* but there is much he doesn't *recognise* (with all the implications of this word). Salk writes:

> One of their main points is that the social world cannot exist on one side and the scientific world on the other because the scientific realm is merely the end result of many other operations that are in the social realm. 'Human affairs' are not different from what the authors call 'scientific production', and the chief accomplishment they claim is to reveal the way in which 'human aspects' are excluded from the final stages of 'fact production'. I have doubts about this way of thinking and, in my own work, find details which do not fit this picture, but I am always stimulated by attempts to show that the two 'cultures' are, in fact, only one. Whatever objection may be raised about the details and by the author's arguments, I am now convinced that this kind of direct examination of scientists at work should be extended and should be encouraged

> by scientists themselves in our own best interest and in the best interest of society.[6]

Not recognising the criteria and knowledge produced by the exogenous values of another discipline – by Latour's anthropology – Salk instead seems to imagine reconstituting Latour's research within the endogenous values of his own discipline. It can be difficult to acknowledge a finding – a truth, data – emanating from a knowledge set or reference points different from one's own. Instead of truly allowing for these differences, Salk looks for a reciprocity, feeling the need to express that the sociologist has gained much from biology. He states a few times in the short introduction that Latour is now informed as much by biology as by anthropology, somehow redressing a perceived imbalance or deficit created by the research into another discipline.[7] Perhaps it is a disciplinary assumption of the 'hard sciences' that there is a single truth and that it is universal. The idea that the two cultures are one may be a function of this disciplinary bias.

Latour's research and Salk's response can be seen as a study in disciplinarity: it is at the site of discourse and language that disciplinary cultural differences are most often enacted. For example, when I introduce Aristotle's *Poetics* to a conference of art practitioners I am met with a rebuttal that ideas from Aristotle don't count as legitimate in these quarters, given his patriarchal views about women and that he was an apologist for slavery.[8] Other philosophical contributions are not usually summarily dismissed on grounds that unacceptability of part renders the whole also unacceptable. This episode demonstrates disciplinarity in the artworld in a way that is reminiscent of Salk's partial recognition of the value of Latour's research, illustrating that some knowledge sources are expunged or simply not recognised. In the same vein, I balk at the seemingly wilful misappropriation by the artworld of the word ontology (and, for that matter, by some anthropologists), when rightfully, according to the discipline of philosophy in which I was trained as an undergraduate, the term epistemology or perhaps 'discourse' should be used.[9] Like Salk and my artworld colleagues at the conference, I also wish to impose the correctness of one discipline on another. The disciplines tussle for authority, assuming the supremacy of their methodology, the precision of their language or the truth of their knowledge. We favour whichever knowledge set, methodology or language we learned as undergraduates. We assume our discipline is more truthful, more correct or more creative and therefore superior, or at least preferable. The cultural theorist Raymond Williams reminds us that language is:

> not a *tradition* to be learned, nor a *consensus* to be accepted, nor a set of meanings which, because it is 'our language' has a natural authority; but as a shaping and reshaping, in real circumstances and from profoundly different and important points of view: a vocabulary to use, to find our own ways in, to change as we find it necessary to change it, as we go on making our own language and history.[10]

With this extract from Williams I am suitably admonished in my desire to purify from art practice the various discipline hybridisations. I am reminded not to expect, or even wish, that artists and anthropologists use words from philosophy as philosophers use them.

Extending an understanding gleaned from the Institutional definition of art and applying it to all academic disciplines, it can be argued that all disciplines are formed by discourse and that they are socially constructed. Traditionally, the point of academic research was understood as increasing the store of knowledge, but it might be more accurate to say that the purpose of research is to create social bonds: 'the notion of an academic *habitus* founded on social exchange, "entertainment value", and productive of *bonhomie* and solidarity', as anthropologist Alfred

Gell describes it.[11] He writes wryly that 'the business of bourgeois anthropologists like me is only to produce texts – or give seminars – directed towards a reception of other anthropologists and interested (metropolitan) parties'.[12] For Gell, the point of research is, above all, social. Being a social anthropologist, this conclusion may simply follow from his disciplinary outlook but it is worth considering, particularly as it reflects the conclusions within the Institutional definition of art.[13]

That knowledge formation is a social process does not diminish its validity or importance and may simply reflect the way social groups work. To say that truth or knowledge formed through disciplines is contingent, partial and not universal is not to say that there are no truths, just that truth is not universal, forever or immutable. Understanding research in this way, we may frame it as a process of adding to, or altering, existing legitimate disciplinary stories, or ways of seeing, or truths. Research might be said to be a process of moving from known stories to new stories; from cliché to nuance, complexity and difference.

Recognising that the ability to contribute is unevenly distributed across a population and depends to some extent on position within a hierarchical structure, and that disciplines are institutional, with centres and margins, we can see how right-wing and hierarchical the idea of disciplinarity can seem. On the other hand, understanding that these centres and margins are not inevitable or natural, and that each contribution is constitutive, subverts this reading. When we understand that centrality and marginality are always the result of specific and discernible mechanisms, we are free to understand our contribution, our position, as we choose. Importantly, one option is to understand our own hand in this process.

Understanding disciplines in this way, we may be able to comprehend disciplinarity in all its limitations and yet maintain a notion of alterity, disruption, rupture. The argument for understanding art as a discipline relies on an understanding of knowledge as disciplinary storytelling. Each discipline has its truths or assumptions, in other words its foundational premises, which were themselves the product of past storytelling. The process occurs to create scientific fact, as in Salk's laboratory, and it also operates on the premise that informs Latour's research. This is also true for art practice. Disciplinary assumptions are the beginnings of new stories that in turn will form future disciplinary assumptions. Disciplinary storytelling reiterates the central stories but it also searches for new stories, or nuanced versions of stories being told. This is what research does. It nuances the orthodox, makes it more complex, or creates new stories from within the rules of the discipline. Art practice, understood as a knowledge-forming discipline, operates in the same way.

Before I describe the discipline of art practice, I must first acknowledge a difference between art practice and other knowledge-forming disciplines. Whether an art practice is understood as offering new or more complex knowledge, as opposed to performing the tropes of orthodoxy and stereotype, may to some extent depend on the context in which it is experienced and the experience of an individual audience member. What is stereotype and cliché for me, an artist with 25 years' professional experience in an artworld informed largely by Anglo-American debates and an Anglo-American canon, inflected by the 'provincial' story of Australian art, is not the same as for someone from, for example, the former Eastern Bloc with formative experience of the art and discourse of the Soviet era. By virtue of my experience with contemporary art made in specific locations and within specific discourses, I will find stereotype and cliché where another may find interesting radicalism. I acknowledge the right of others to experience the type of art that I find stereotypical – an example of the endless variations on a basic matrix – as interesting or affective. I am not attempting to close down the experience of art for others or to create a hierarchy of aesthetic values to which all right-minded others (people like me) should adhere. Instead, I am trying to describe a set of endogenous values that artists can share and a set of values that we must attempt to articulate if we are to resist the full internalisation and embodiment of neoliberalism.

The disciplinarity of art practice

Archaeologist Colin Renfrew has made a study of modern and contemporary art, comparing it to archaeology. Contributing to two books on the subject and curating a programme of contemporary art for Jesus College, University of Cambridge, Renfrew has considered the subject from a point of view that embraces human prehistory and acknowledges the specificities of time and place. He claims that the task of archaeology is the same as reading contemporary art and that 'this is no analogy'.[14] He writes that:

> Today the visual arts have transformed themselves into what might be described as a vast, uncoordinated yet somehow enormously effective research programme that looks critically at what we are and how we know what we are – at the foundations of knowledge and perception, and of the structures that modern societies have chosen to construct upon these foundations.[15]

Though Renfrew refers to but a small segment of the contemporary artworld, focusing mostly on object-based art in public collections, his statement about the role and ambition of contemporary art is cogent. He constructs a way of understanding the achievement of art, not in terms of aesthetics, process or materials but in terms of knowledge. He goes on to explain:

> Artists do their own thing and may well reject assignment to an allotted place in a 'research programme' however uncoordinated. But archaeology also has its research programme, which again is not coordinated by any central national or supranational agency. Over the past half-century we have, for instance, learnt much more about the origins of food production worldwide, through well-focused programmes of research on different continents. No one has coordinated this research, but it has achieved a certain coherence through the independent scrutiny of the work of one researcher by another. That is how science works: results are published and assessed, and go on to influence the work of others. To some extent this is true also in the visual arts.[16]

Renfrew compares art to the academic disciplines of science and archaeology, which are based on peer-review, disciplinary rules of the game and a history of that discipline.

If art practice is a type of research programme, it is important to differentiate between the type of research undertaken within art practice and, say, that done by an archaeologist or an anthropologist.[17] This difference is not just in terms of the output, where one is visual and the other text. Anthropologists today use poetry, film, photography and other art forms to convey their data. Sometimes, they produce very interesting art-like creations.[18] By contrast, many artists write and use text in their work, even writing books, for example, or mimicking the methodologies of anthropology or archaeology. But it is the knowledge sets that are different, unique to each discipline, as are the values and norms guiding production. For example, an anthropological film such as *Sweetgrass* (2009) must in the first instance satisfy the criteria of anthropology for it to be considered as anthropology.[19] The research process itself, as well as the types of questions raised by the various disciplines, are different even when their 'products' or 'outputs' superficially seem to share similar qualities. *Sweetgrass*, however artistically interesting and despite being distributed through art venues such as the ICA, is unlikely to be considered art even if its makers or distributors wish this to be the case. The process of recategorisation or double categorisation is not done by the author or practitioner but by its recipients, as the artefact or practice becomes part of the knowledge reproduced and disseminated through discipline-specific channels.

Colin Renfrew writes warmly about the artist Mark Dion, stating that, in addition to making art that references archaeological processes, he has actually made a contribution to archaeological knowledge.[20] I have no doubt that Dion is chuffed about this fact, but I doubt that producing archaeological knowledge continues to be an ambition for him; his knowledge set, reference points and ambitions lie with the discipline of art and not the discipline of archaeology.

There is a naivety to Colin Renfrew's statement about contemporary art practice as a type of research programme. He proposes that art practice can be understood as a knowledge-forming discipline involved in an unstructured research programme, just as archaeology is. For his purposes, Renfrew has no need of a philosophy of art or art theory and he does not offer his views on art from a philosopher's disciplinary bias or knowledge set. He is not required to engage with or refute those, such as John Dewey, who write explicitly that art is not a mode of knowledge. According to Dewey, art is something far more valuable than knowledge in that it enables the experience of experience.[21] What is important about Dewey's argument against art as knowledge is that he demonstrates the problem in defining knowledge in the first place, and it is useful to be aware of assumptions within its definition. Dewey restricts the idea of knowledge to its narrower sense, as the type of intellectual and cerebral knowledge that the discipline of philosophy most often produces. In his argument he cites Wordsworth and Shelley and their ideas about art as a form of knowledge, but he dismisses them saying that they are 'speaking imaginatively':

> Wordsworth declared that 'poetry is the breath and finer spirit of all knowledge; it is the impassioned expression which is in the countenance of all science.' Shelley said: 'Poetry is at once the center and circumference of all knowledge; it is that which comprehends all science and to which all science must be referred.' But these men were poets and are speaking imaginatively ... far from being knowledge in any literal sense ... And Shelley also says, 'poetry awakens and enlarges the mind by rendering it the receptacle of a thousand unapprehended combinations of thought.' I cannot find in such remarks as these any intention to assert that esthetic experience is to be *defined* as a mode of knowledge. What is intimated to my mind, is, that in both production and enjoyed perception of works of art, knowledge is transformed; it becomes something more than knowledge because it is merged with non-intellectual elements to form an experience worthwhile as an experience.[22]

This passage seems once again to demonstrate the disciplinarity of disciplines. The philosopher claims the authority to define knowledge and disregards the artists' views. Wordsworth and Shelley know that art creates knowledge, that art is knowledge-forming. Without pinning down the type of knowledge produced, like the poets I also maintain that art does produce a type of knowledge and, more importantly for this chapter, that art practice is a knowledge-forming discipline akin to any other knowledge-forming discipline.

As a knowledge-forming discipline, the history of art practice has its origins with the beginning of the modern era, with what Foucault describes as the era of liberal self-governance. This is distinct from the history of art objects, which is considerably longer in its current definition as it includes the 40,000-year-old 'rock art' found in various locations in Australia.

The current definition of art objects includes objects from times and cultures that I am excluding here from the idea of art practice as a discipline, which I define specifically as a modern practice. I am making a distinction between most of what is understood as art within the Institutional definition of art and the discipline of art practice, because though the definition of art is expansive and open, the discipline of art has a much shorter history and one that is intertwined with the history of the modern era. For example, that produced in the medieval period or by 'pre-contact' Australian Aboriginal people may be art, but it is not a modern art practice. Here I am not reiterating those twentieth-century arguments about who it is that makes art as compared with craft or magic or any other denigrated category of creative production.[23] For many traditional art historians, the Renaissance emphasis on the expression of individual sensibility or genius marks out an art practice, but here disciplinary art practice is not defined as the expression of individual genius or subjectivity.[24] Disciplinary art practice is understood specifically as the material and intellectual negotiation with, and performance of, the conditions of modernity. Renaissance art was made for different reasons, within different parameters and values, including the fact that art products then had an assured place in society, being part of church and aristocratic patronage. During the Renaissance, art was a reflection and negotiation with the values and mechanisms of the *Ancien Régime*. Here the discipline of art practice is defined as a willed, conscious response to its conditions, negotiating and performing its modernity. The discipline of art emerged from negotiating and performing the conditions of the modern era and it began, like many other disciplines including science, with the Enlightenment.

It is Raymond Williams' *Keywords* that supports the idea that both art practice and science began with the Enlightenment. He demonstrates that the word aesthetic was only introduced into English in the nineteenth century and was not in common usage or associated directly with art before the mid-nineteenth century. It was first used in Latinate form in the mid-eighteenth century as *aesthetica* by the German philosopher Alexander Baumgarten, a contemporary of Kant. The idea of aesthetics must, therefore, be understood as an Enlightenment concept, a product of modernity, not even wholly associated with fine art for another hundred years. The word art itself, as used here, only entered common language in the nineteenth century, though with some eighteenth-century precedents.[25] The modern definition of science also dates back to the nineteenth century; the *Oxford English Dictionary* dates the origin of the word scientist to 1834. It is more commonly understood that science had its origins in the Enlightenment whereas art, even as we understand it, is imagined to have ancient origins. Science historian Simon Schaffer problematises the idea of a 200-year-old history of modern science. His argument is that in the mythologising process that creates a discipline's history, what is heterogeneous and messy is rendered homogenous.[26] Inevitably, a discipline's historical storytelling is simplified in retrospect and this has been problematic for the story of science. I would argue, though, that there is a clear distinction before and after the modern period in what was done in the name of art as well as science. Changes in rationale or supporting discourses link art's disciplinary beginnings and processes with those of other knowledge-forming disciplines to the Enlightenment or modern period.

Modernity, meaning specifically the end of the *Ancien Régime* with its system of autocratic rule and aristocratic patronage, and the beginning of the era of liberal self-governance with its emphasis on the individual as agent and technology of power, meant fundamentally a new negotiation with power, knowledge and commerce. The inception of the Society for the Encouragement of Arts, Manufactures and Commerce in the mid-eighteenth century seems to embody this negotiation within the new regime; a negotiated engagement with capitalism, technology and art emerged at the same historical moment. Now called simply the RSA implying a stress on the arts, it has not lost its longer title of the Society for the Encouragement of Arts, Manufactures and Commerce. Notably, the Society was also the precursor to the Royal Academy (RA).

Art practice can be considered a discipline in that its purpose is to create and police knowledge and that its history is similar to the history of those disciplines that were born of modernity. The history of art practice may, therefore, be understood as comparable to the history of other late eighteenth- and nineteenth-century disciplines such as science, archaeology and anthropology; it is only then that modern ideas about art in the abstract emerge.[27] Art practice is a response to the conditions of modernity understood and guided by the Enlightenment 'principle of critique and a permanent creation of ourselves in our autonomy',[28] as Foucault describes it, appreciating the Enlightenment legacy as positive with the proviso that we also understand that this does not imply an embrace of Enlightenment humanism and 'its specific theological and metaphysical conception of human nature'.[29]

In common with other disciplines, art practice has its own history of thought and historiography, a set of both established and outmoded methodologies, and a set of reference points to which practitioners orientate themselves. Each discipline has core knowledge and core practitioners to which all within that discipline must be acquainted. Each discipline has a lexicon that undergraduates or novitiates must learn in order to be taken seriously, in order to be 'heard' or to be understood as professional, as worth listening to. The language of a discipline also serves to exclude, as in medicine where doctors may talk over the heads of a patient, both literally and metaphorically. The use of discipline-specific language is the same in all disciplines, including art. It is an effective and important way of establishing who is 'us' and who is 'them'; who is professional and who is included. Disciplines have histories – and histories that relate those changing histories. They have a self-consciousness about their history while claiming that in the present we have learned from the past (and now, therefore, it is all different somehow). Each discipline is the product of its history or, more accurately, its historiography. There are also core methodologies within disciplines. For example, in medicine, it is dissection; in anthropology, field work; in archaeology, the dig. In art practice, it was life drawing whereas now it is discursive: being able to talk about one's art or curatorial practice in discipline-specific terms.

Artists work within a body of knowledge. This knowledge includes other artists' work, art sites and hierarchies of eminence. To a lesser extent, it also includes theories and histories of art. To be an art practitioner, one must have knowledge not of medium or tools, but of the work of other key artists plus the most conspicuous institutional systems (important galleries, curators, names, places). Disciplines are not defined by their processes or materials. They are defined by their knowledge sets and their methodologies – and these are policed by adherents. Because they are policed, they also periodically have crises. This is as true of art practice as of any other discipline. These are not crises in practice, but in definition and legitimacy.

Described like this, disciplines seem petty and arbitrary, potentially getting in the way of knowledge (or truth, beauty, etc.). The philosopher-historian G. E. R. Lloyd, in books published in 2007 and 2009, examined various disciplines across cultures and periods.[30] He was interested in the assumptions that happen when we map disciplines, or ways of seeing, on to other cultures and other times. His analysis was done by a cross-cultural comparison of eight disciplines: philosophy, mathematics, history, medicine, art, law, religion and science, starting from his own lifelong research comparing ancient Greece with ancient China. Not only does he observe that experts tend to police their discipline, having crises or controversies when boundaries are breached, but that this process is confined neither to modern times nor to complex societies. With the final paragraph of his second book, Lloyd concludes that:

> [there is a] constant, or as [Thomas] Kuhn (1977) called it essential tension between innovation and authority, though the histories we have charted suggest that it is scarcely possible to secure the advantages of the one without the disadvantages associated with the other.[31]

There are definite disadvantages to the disciplining of knowledge, which boil down to their rigidity and the fixity imposed by authority. This is the ubiquitous and, arguably, necessary policing of disciplines: their methods, languages, knowledge sets, their boundaries and even who are the legitimated practitioners. Crises will inevitably occur whenever this authority is challenged but we can rely on the fact that, as Lloyd describes, authorities will always be challenged over time and in all societies, be they simple or complex. Innovation, newness and change are products of disciplinarity. The eminent anthropologist Marilyn Strathern makes a similar point with respect to debates about interdisciplinarity, in that it is the *disciplines* that continue to sustain intellectual change because they foster productive forms of internal disagreement and dissent and that 'the value of a discipline is precisely in its ability to account for its conditions of existence and thus ... how it arrives at its knowledge practices'.[32]

In understanding that innovation is the product of disciplinarity, it becomes important to distance the idea from two problematic associations. The first is a teleological implication, present in both Christianity and (ironically) some interpretations of Darwinian evolutionary theory. The second problematic association is with capitalism.

A driving narrative within both Christianity and evolutionary theory is innovation, change, newness. Both systems of thought perceive time as a type of journey – and innovation and change are markers on this journey. One journey, the Christian journey, goes from bad to good; the other, the evolutionary journey, goes from simplicity to complexity, where these states carry the implication of inferiority and superiority respectively, as racist evolutionary theory explicates. It is important to realise that this journey trope is only one way of perceiving time and experience. With Christianity, the tale of humanity is the procession from bad to good, enacted since Adam's fall from grace, embodied in each individual's struggle with God: if an individual is to achieve immortal life, they must journey from bad (original sin) to good. Evolutionary theory has a similar emphasis on journeying from bad to good. Some narrate the tale of evolution as a progression from simple to complex with 'bad' traits or genes shed along the way. Although this teleological narration is strictly extraneous to evolutionary theory, it often surfaces: the creatures alive today are understood as superior, having apparently triumphed with better genetic material as compared with creatures now extinct. The other problematic association with the concept of innovation has emerged from a capitalist narrative. In this tale, innovation is instrumentalised for profit. Innovation is understood as good when it increases or consolidates profit and, as Boltanski and Chiapello have shown, innovation is itself a capitalist trope.

The nuance and complexities of disciplinary innovation that are valued here have neither teleological nor instrumentalist overtones. Instead, innovation is valuable in a discipline's endogenous terms. Innovation is the creation of new stories, new ways of seeing – nuances and complexities that move the discipline, and sometimes wider society, away from orthodoxy. This is valuable not just because complexity and nuance may in itself be preferable to orthodoxy but because nuanced, complex ways of seeing are beneficial to wider society in social and political terms. This will be described more fully in the next chapter.

There is an inherent tension within disciplines between innovation and authority, but not only does the artworld actually work in this way whether it acknowledges this or not, what art practitioners gain from art's disciplinarity – from its institutional recognition – is a licence to behave in specific ways that are understood in one or all of the following terms: free, creative, innovative, open, sincere, authentic, individual, organic, different, original. We have this licence by virtue of art's institutional authority as a discipline. The disciplining of knowledge has both advantages and disadvantages but, if G. E. R. Lloyd is right, they are ubiquitous and we, as discipline constituents, contribute to them both from the margins and from the core.

Points to note

There are a few clarifications regarding art as a knowledge-forming discipline.

First, the distinction between art as intellectual property and art as a knowledge-forming discipline; second, the distinction between art as a knowledge-forming discipline and that made within research programmes as academic research; third, the idea of art as a praxis as distinct from activism, education or other praxes. These are discussed below.

Art as intellectual property and art as a knowledge-forming discipline

When I write of art as a discipline I emphatically do not mean art in its newest guise as part of the knowledge economy, as intellectual property, as part of the institutionalisation of all forms of (useful) knowledge. That so many artists, curators and artworld theorists understand the idea of knowledge in the first instance in terms of intellectual property, the knowledge economy or the instrumentalised and measurable forms is another indicator of how far neoliberal values have penetrated the artworld.

Interestingly, there is a debate around 'interdisciplinarity', ongoing for more than ten years, that exists in the social sciences. In that debate, the idea of disciplinary knowledge, which is 'autonomous' (meaning free from government and market interference), is opposed to interdisciplinary knowledge, which suffers from all the pitfalls described earlier of marketisation and instrumentalisation. It is argued that it is disciplinarity itself that serves as a bulwark against neoliberalism.[33] Social scientists Georgina Born and Andrew Barry, who work in this field, have argued that the notion of invention, and specifically invention in terms of knowledge, points to the openness (or otherwise) of a contemporary historical situation. For Born and Barry, invention must be understood as the introduction of a form of novelty within a specific domain that serves 'to protend or open up the space of future possibilities'.[34]

Art as knowledge-forming discipline vs. academic research

Some contemporary art is made as part of self-conscious 'practice-led research' and 'measured' by academic institutions and academic funders. In writing about art as a discipline, I am not promoting the academicisation of art practice, as has happened in the UK over the past 30 years. In Ivan Illich's *Deschooling Society* (1971) referring to education in general, he writes of an 'arms race' for academic qualifications that does little for society or for knowledge, or for an individual's sense of empowerment. Instead the arms race does a great job maintaining those hierarchical institutions offering qualifications (plus a passive, subservient and consumerist status quo).[35] There has been an increasing 'academicisation' of art practice in the UK, meaning a proliferation of increasingly higher degrees of qualification. In previous generations, most artists had no university qualification and none was *required* to be an artist. Art schools were yet to be part of the university system. Even today, many contemporary artists from an older generation have no formal or university qualifications; instead they became artists through their practice.[36] Today, not only is art practice an academic discipline fit for doctoral research, but the role of curator in contemporary art galleries and in many commissioning bodies tends to be taken up by those with Master of Arts degrees in curating. In the past, curators or directors of contemporary art galleries had no such qualification, as none existed. Galleries with historical collections were headed up by those with degrees in art history. No longer is it possible, as it once was for a person to learn a job or to master a discipline through experience and mentoring alone. Universities have stepped in to maintain and normalise a process of standardisation. This process has been critiqued by various parties within the artworld as a further aspect of encroaching neoliberalism.[37] I hope it is clear that it is not this kind of discipline that I am advocating here.

Art as praxis

In addition to art being understood as a discipline, a system of thought and knowledge production, it must also be understood as a type of action, hence a praxis. I am aware that this is not the traditional usage of the word praxis. As political theorist Paolo Virno explains, 'Praxis is ordinarily understood as distinct from both Action and from Intellect where praxis is Politics.'[38] Here I conflate the term so that the idea of praxis includes action and intellect. By understanding the term in this way, art becomes one of the few praxis disciplines, the others being education, activism and perhaps psychotherapy. Defined as conscious, willed action informed by theory or philosophy and transformed into a materialised social activity, praxis is ordinarily understood within political revolutionary terms. The type of praxis I am advocating here, however, is not a revolutionary one. If art is understood as a praxis it must be understood as distinct from the other two praxes of education and political activism into which it has recently been folded.

Art is not activism nor is it education. To imagine art practice in terms of either is to do a disservice to art, to activism and to education. They each have different goals and knowledge sets, even when they share methodologies and reference points and even when these differences are not recognised. Some of the confusion may lie in an increasing emphasis on creativity in both education and activism and it is laudable that both activism and education are increasingly creative in their methodologies, but as every business person will tell you, echoing Boltanski and Chiapello's thesis, capitalism too is creative.[39] Art practice is not simply the enactment of creativity and it has no monopoly on creativity or on creative uses of material or methodology. It is true that some types of activism use creative performance techniques derived from art practice, techniques invented by the Situationist International (1957–69) such as *détournement.*[40] Some activists refer to art history and admire artists such as Joseph Beuys and Hans Haacke. This is a process of inspiration and, perhaps, diffusion. However, the inspiration of activists by historical art practices doesn't alter the specificity of activism or the specificity of art practice. Mirroring this process of diffusion, some artists read political theorists such as

Hannah Arendt or educationalists such as Paolo Freire, but the focus and knowledge set within which we operate is art practice. That disciplines rely on models and paradigms borrowed from each other was observed by Michel de Certeau in his project to exacerbate the fragmentation of knowledge in order to demonstrate that disciplines are 'constructed'.[41] But pointing out that disciplines share paradigms and models hardly undermines the argument for disciplinarity, it just states that they have interconnected influences, perhaps because of the diffusion of knowledge or paradigms. The point I want to stress is that to imagine that the different praxes of art, activism and education are on some sort of a continuum because they sometimes share reference points or methodologies is to undermine the importance and unique contribution of each and to misunderstand how disciplinarity operates.

Disciplinary difference as cultural difference

Having described the acquisition of disciplinarity through education and the idea that disciplines become schema onto which adult experience is mapped, it might be possible to compare the differences that ensue between disciplines to a subtle form of cultural difference. In distinguishing between art and other activity, we therefore face the challenge of difference. Philosopher Emmanuel Levinas, for whom the elision of difference was unethical, conceptualises difference, the Other, philosophically and he requires of us an ethical engagement with the other as Other.[42] For Levinas, the problem begins with the fact that Western knowledge is based on an ancient Greek episteme, with an ongoing assumption about universality and knowledge so that, in this tradition, we have inherited an unacknowledged but alarming paradox. Knowledge is understood as universal and yet knowledge stems from, and is confined to, the particularity of the Greco-European experience and tradition. Based on *philia*, a system of likeness, or the exchange of the Same with the Same, this system of knowledge inherently has a horror of the Other. This horror can only be minimised when the Other is assimilated as part of the Same. The other is not allowed to be Other, but instead is an extension of the Self, the Same. Examples of this type of extension of the Same, can be seen in Orientalism or Primitivism – where a culture, a person or a cultural artefact is not understood on its own terms but as part of what is already 'understood' or imagined of that culture. This is unethical in Levinasian terms.

Thinking back to the origins of this book and the inspiration for these thoughts, before any real encounter with activists, I had imagined they were the same as me, as a politically aware, socially engaged artist, but experience exposed differences in our knowledge sets, methodologies, assumptions and language. These disciplinary differences do not exist when I meet other contemporary artists in cultures different from my own. As artists we share a common set of assumptions, reference points and knowledge sets that I do not share with activists from London. To erase the difference between the culture of the artworld and the culture of activism, to imagine they are part of a continuum, seems unethical in a Levinasian sense: it imposes a culture of the Same on the Other, not recognising Difference, except as extension of the Same.

One of the differences between politics and art can be seen in the methods and goals of the political. Politics specifically is to *act on*, or *with*, the multitude. The guru or leader model acts *on* the multitude, winning the mass of hearts and minds, usually from a position of privilege, from the front or the top. As much as the model is resisted, traditional democratic party politics work with this model, as does much traditional activism – such as the Trades Union movement – and non-traditional activism.

In contrast, working *with* the multitude is collaborative, forming networks of interest groups and altering systems through participation. As its locus is the multitude, politics is not individualised, nor should it be. Hardt and Negri explicitly admonish that politics is not singular. In the passage on refusal in *Empire*, they warn against the smallness of singular resistance; the fact that, while it is possible and it may be symbolically beautiful, singular resistance has no political efficacy.[43]

One of the most important characteristics of an art praxis is that art's focus is on the self or selves, and not the other, the mass or the multitude. To state that art practice begins with the self as distinct from activism or education is not to judge art ill, but to clarify inherent differences that go beyond knowledge set or methodology. Art enacts the individual negotiation with discourse, power, knowledge. Its concern is agency, complexity of the self and nuancing stories or orthodoxies. This is as true of a collaborative artwork as it is of an individual's. Art practice is therefore radically different from activism and education. To focus on the individual here is not to depoliticise, but instead to emphasise individual agency within systems of power. Art, understood as both praxis and singular, retains its political importance in a society that values freedom and resistance, where we believe that freedom and resistance must originate in the individual. In this sense, Allan Kaprow's lifelike art typifies an art praxis as much as Donald Judd's artlike art.

Michel de Certeau writes that all knowledge is historiographic storytelling, that 'storytelling has a pragmatic efficacy. In pretending to recount the real, it manufactures it. It is performative. … In making believers, it produces an active body of practitioners.'[44] This is the importance of art as a discipline. We do not tell stories as solipsistic acts, working in garrets, ahead of our time and waiting to be discovered – as the Romantic myth has it. We constitute both our discipline and, more importantly, the stories of our time, performing them.

There is a distinction to be made between the disruptive potential of art and simply being against. A ubiquitous 'being against', as some suggest, is a strategy generative of opposition, of *no* to *yes* and *yes* to *no*.[45] However, it is not a strategy that opens up many, multiple, various, nuanced, complex, other stories, being predefined against something else. Instead, the discipline of art can, and sometimes does, open up and enact this type of new story. Potentially it creates a breach in normative discourse, rupturing the sensorium as Rancière would say, or creating, in the words of Michel de Certeau, when describing the contribution of Foucault:

> bouts of surprise ... the sudden jubilatory, semi-ecstatic forms of 'astonishment' or 'wonder' ... Something that exceeds the thinkable and opens the possibility of 'thinking otherwise' bursts in through comical incongruous or paradoxical half-opening through discourse. The philosopher, overtaken by laughter, seized by an irony of things equivalent to an illumination, is not the author but the witness of these flashes traversing and transgressing the gridding of discourses effected by established systems of reason ... This surprising inventiveness of words and things, this intellectual experience of a disappropriation that opens possibilities, is what Foucault marks with a laugh. It is his philosophical signature on the irony of history.[46]

In other words, like other disciplinary forms of new knowledge/storytelling, art may produce the kind of surprises that profoundly alter our established ways of seeing. This is not to confuse deep irony and rupture with the trite irony peddled by the art market and advertisers. The irony here is comparable instead to a mudslide where the very terrain alters, reconfiguring the foundations of knowledge and understanding.

An endogenous value of art

The artist creates an experience for an audience through a painting, a sculpture, an exhibition, a photograph, an installation, a live event, a website, a performance, a film, a collaboration, an intervention. In creating an artwork, an artist has in mind a history of similar 'experience-experiments', which include their own artwork, other artworks directly in their field of 'research' and, more widely, key moments or figures in the discipline of art. The artist may be said, therefore, to be in dialogue with the past as they create artworks in the present for future audiences. It is a knowing, conscious act with intentions that are, in the first place, a response to a personal trajectory within the discipline. Only secondarily is an artwork a response to a market, a commissioning brief, an exhibition opportunity.

The idea of disciplinarity answers the need expressed by ongoing artworld discussion around valuing art practice in terms other than the market. The idea of art as a knowledge-forming discipline helps to articulate a set of endogenous values for art practice that are distinct from the market. These values may overlap, or they may not. For example, Damien Hirst's entire oeuvre is being sold at hyper-inflated prices as a consequence of its being valued by the art market as art, as distinct from any other type of product. But his artworks fall into two categories: art and not art. Some of his art practice contributes to art as a knowledge-forming discipline and some does not. His gold butterfly constructions and spin paintings, for example, however pretty, offer no new, nuanced or more complex stories or ways of seeing within the knowledge created through the discipline of art. It is not that they are mere commodities or that they have an inherent relationship with the market that makes them not-art in disciplinary terms, it is that these objects offer nothing but tired cliché, reproducing not just the neoliberal grid of commoditisation (applying the abstract principle that commodification should exist at all levels, in all aspects of society), but a reductive simplification of art practice and a repetitive reiteration of this banality. They therefore have little value in terms of the discipline of art practice. This is not to dismiss all of Hirst's oeuvre. Other of his artworks have created new stories, new ways of seeing and, therefore, they are art and are valuable as art in the disciplinary sense. The idea of disciplinarity in art practice helps to describe the difference between the trite and banal, and the nuanced and complex. Disciplinarity helps to articulate the value of a discipline, whatever its intersection with market values or the distortions created when understanding value only through the prism of neoliberalism.

If artworks are to be understood as having a value that is endogenous, outside the market and neoliberal norms (or, for that matter, any other totalising discourse), we must subject them to the discipline of disciplinarity. That which adds to art's store of knowledge becomes exemplary of the discipline and is the standard. All artworks 'tell stories', sometimes literally, and at other times, metaphorically. Piet Mondrian, Arshile Gorky and Eva Hesse tell one type of story about colour, composition, balance, line, form. Hans Haacke, Rirkrit Tiravanija and Sonia Boyce tell another type about relationships, power and visibility. What makes all their art exemplary in disciplinary terms, across art–life binaries, is that their stories are more nuanced or more complicated than the stories that came before, and that each artist created these stories in response to a knowledge of the history of art practice.

At this moment in time, different parts of the artworld champion different types of art practice. The art market tends to favour the art that plays with form or self-consciously subverts genre, while the biennial market favours art that more overtly works in the lifelike tradition. In neither the biennial market nor the auction house market – with their separate but honed discourses – is there an overarching rationale for the question of what is art, let alone what is good art. Without this, the inclusions and exclusions are fairly arbitrary, simply the enactment of power as described by Gielen and network theory (Chapter 2). Without an overall rationale that articulates value, except by association with networks of power, the artworld operates crudely as power and ultimately allows the values of neoliberalism to dominate. This is as true of the less funded or self-supported part of the artworld. This is why a story of art's value that links the various fractures within the contemporary artworld is important, including all types of practice equally, while making distinctions between the interesting and the mediocre, between art and not-art.

Conclusion

Ever since motorcycles and Armani clothing were exhibited in museums, they and the large institutional galleries no longer have the same *de facto* authority to define art as they once did. Not everything that is seen in a gallery can now be understood as art. Clothes and machines do not become art just because they are exhibited in the Guggenheim museums and experienced as objects of aesthetic contemplation. Motorcycles and clothing are commercial products, made primarily as commodities and not as art, but this fact is not the reason these objects are not art. They are not art specifically because they were not made with the history and knowledge set of art practice in mind. The same is true of activism or education when it is experienced in art galleries. Neither education nor activism is art just because it is experienced in a gallery. When the 'C Words' exhibition, curated by PLATFORM, the creative activist organisation, was seen at the Arnolfini gallery in Bristol in 2009, the experience was interesting and important, but it was not art. Like Armani, PLATFORM's points of reference, knowledge base and methodologies do not lie within the discipline of art. It is the history, knowledge base and praxes of activism and education that inform PLATFORM's work. Like the Guggenheim exhibitions, the context of the Arnolfini does not alter the fact that 'C Words' was something other than art.

This is a non-hierarchical observation. To be not-art does not equate necessarily to an idea of inferiority. To be art is not to be superior, though the term is used metaphorically to convey excellence: his *couture* is so splendid it is like art. Asserting difference is often seen as claiming superiority, or inferiority. I am arguing for distinctiveness without hierarchy. I do not police the boundary of art so that I may inscribe for myself a position of power but in order to examine and celebrate what art is and how it is distinct from other types of practices, praxes, disciplines, actions. In previous chapters I have argued against binaries. This was not simply to fulfil the postmodern imperative of collapsing all dichotomies but in order to raze the conceptual ground, to return a reflexivity to the artworld and one that has resistant or disruptive potential for this moment.

CHAPTER 6
In Conclusion

Summary

I have argued that an endogenous value for art must be found and that this lies in the concept of disciplinarity because, despite disciplines and institutions being agents of orthodoxy, they are also agents of innovation, crisis and change. The point of knowledge-forming disciplines, in addition to defining and policing their ground, is to create new, nuanced or more complex stories because it is this that constitutes new knowledge. New disciplinary knowledge interrogates orthodoxies and puts in their place new stories, which themselves later become orthodoxies against which to tell new and nuanced stories. Because of the problematic association with both capitalism and modernist myths of genius, the artworld has rightfully become suspicious of newness and innovation. Consequently, we have lost the ability to articulate what comprises interesting or excellent art, instead leaving that to the market and to opaque artworld networks that rely on arbitrary consensus in the absence of any endogenous artworld values that are shared and open. By creating, promulgating and inhabiting stories from within a different set of values – producing nuance and complexity in the face of orthodoxy – the artworld will be better able to resist totalising discourses, including neoliberalism. This is true of all disciplines, but because art is not just a knowledge-forming discipline but a public action, entailing both action and story, it is directly constitutive of the public realm. Stories constitute ourselves, our personal and public identities, our society. When art enacts plurality, it necessarily makes the simplistic, reductive orthodoxies more nuanced and more complicated. By doing so, art makes possible further nuance and complexity. At times, in addition, art articulates and embodies another way of seeing, not simply restating a binary opposite (itself a cliché), but profoundly disrupting of the order of things.

◆ ◆ ◆ ◆

> The politics of art suffers from a strange schizophrenia ... they say we must completely re-think the politics of art ... [yet] these very same artists and critics are still very attached to paradigms for understanding the efficacy of art that were debunked at least two centuries before ... We may no longer believe that exhibiting virtues and vices on stage can improve human behaviour, but we continue to act as if reproducing a commercial idol in resin will engender resistance against the 'spectacle', and as if a series of photographs about the way colonisers represent the colonised will work to undermine the fallacies of mainstream representations of identities ... These sorts of rhetorical *dispositif* still prevail in a good many galleries and museums professing to be revealing the power of the commodity, the reign of the spectacle or the pornography of power. But since it is very difficult to find anybody who is actually ignorant of such things, the mechanism ends up spinning around itself and playing on the very undecidability of its effect. In the end, the *dispositif* feeds off the very equivalence between parody *as* critique and the parody of critique.[1]
>
> *Jacques Rancière,* Dissensus: On Politics and Aesthetics

◆ ◆ ◆ ◆

> ... from the idea that the self is not given to us, I think that there is only one practical consequence: we have to create ourselves as a work of art.[2]
>
> *Michel Foucault, 'On the Genealogy of Ethics'*

◆ ◆ ◆ ◆

That we live with newly pernicious structures of power, understood as neoliberalism, is much discussed in many parts of the artworld. This book has added to that discussion by bringing in further examples of neoliberal mechanisms manifested within artworld structures and by looking at the values that have been inculcated across the spectrum of the artworld, from the monied end to the self-funded. Different parts of the artworld have different relationships to politics and to commercialism, as has been the case from the beginning of modernity, but today the vast majority of practitioners, including the most radical, now harbour values that even where not overtly commercial, follow neoliberal imperatives that replicate the norms and values of the market, such as measurement and populism. Neoliberal mechanisms, such as self-responsibilisation, were described by Foucault as the mechanisms of power operating from the era of liberal self-governance, but with the rise of neoliberalism and the specific monetary policies that implemented Milton Friedman's vision for capitalism in the 1980s, Foucault's observations have even more urgent implications. The model of power Foucault describes is distinct from a traditional Marxist model of power in that power is not imagined in binary terms, where classes of people have power or otherwise and the powerful set about finding ever more novel ways of oppressing everyone else. Instead, Foucault describes a model of power in which wherever we are positioned in the hierarchical structures of society, we each self-manage, having absorbed interests and desires that replicate and embody the structures of power, of society. We do this because it is in our desires, our interests, our knowledge and perception, and not just because we *imagine* it is in our interests: 'We never desire against our interests, because interest always follows and finds itself where desire has placed it.'[3]

Various binaries consequent of a binary model of power continue to have resonance in the contemporary artworld, underlining the fact that a binary model fuels the artworld imagination, despite near-ubiquitous references to Foucault, postmodernism and more recent theorists urging us to conceive the artworld in non-binary terms. Clearly our interests seem to remain with the binary model or we would imagine and inhabit differently. One such interest and its product is the idea of authenticity. This concept has deep resonance for artists in the modern era and the value of authenticity is reproduced both in the market and in Marxist thought. In the market-orientated part of the artworld, the authentic–inauthentic binary is typified by the art of Tracey Emin, where authenticity is understood along the humanist lines that Sartre expounded and which are critiqued above. The market justifies this type of authentic–inauthentic binary by claiming to reward what is authentic, the product of an authentically troubled or inspired genius, prizing an apparent authenticity, or a lack of inauthenticity, understood in Romantic terms. Paradoxically, with postmodernism and neoliberalism, the market also values inauthenticity: series made as self-conscious artist-brands by, for example, Hirst and Takashi Murakami, and the mechanically reproduced that can potentially recur in limitless editions (digital media but also more traditional printmaking can be even more valuable on the market as a series than a single painting or sculpture[4]). In addition, the non- or anti-commercial part of the artworld also has a tendency to echo Sartre's notion of authenticity. There is a strand within the Marxist tradition where authenticity is prized in contradistinction to market values, opposed to capitalist or bourgeois values. Marxist art theorist, Adolfo Sánchez Vázquez typifies this view :

> The artist is wealthy, not in the material sense – the only admissible value in modern political economy – but as a social being who feels an impulse to realise his essence. Inasmuch as man has created himself by affirming himself in the objective world through his labour, the measures of his wealth are powers of expression and objectification. [Quoting Marx:] 'The rich human being is ... the man in whom his own realisation exists as an inner necessity, as need.'[5]

Marxist authenticity draws on the idea of a self that exists outside market and other values imagined to be exogenous. The authentic–inauthentic binary is not only problematic simply because it replicates flawed binary models of power that ultimately render us either impotent or omnipotent, but because notions of authenticity and inauthenticity prevent us from understanding the point that Foucault makes when he writes that 'from the idea that the self is not given to us, I think that there is only one practical consequence: we have to create ourselves as a work of art'.[6] Just as a work of art is an act of creation, so too is the self. By understanding the self as an act of creation, not a whole or constant being which is either authentic or inauthentic, and art as one type of creation, art can be understood as having a uniquely important role in understanding the idea of the self. Art can instantiate the idea of the self as creation.

Working within a binary model of power, the artworld tends to promote a model that assumes the presence of good guys and bad guys, plus a range of assumed good practices, modes of display, sites and media. These are examples of some of the many artworld orthodoxies. Artworld novitiates learn what is acceptable and desirable in art and about the artworld structures that reward adherence to artworld norms. Sometimes students also learn the history of why these norms and values are desirable but we are not taught to question these orthodoxies because, by its own definition, the artworld allegedly does not contain orthodoxies. Because the idea of orthodoxy implies institutions, disciplines, policing boundaries of inclusion and exclusion, and hierarchy, the artworld prefers to imagine we don't have them, which itself has led to the orthodoxy that everyone is an artist and that anything an artist says is art is art. When the artworld does admit the presence of orthodoxies, they are imagined to lie solely with those who work in the artlike tradition.

Understanding that power operates (replicated and enacted) through our interests, our desire, our bodies and our knowledge, this book is an attempt at altering our understanding of self-interest, self-definition and desire. It proposes that we really attempt to understand the binary operations that have informed practice throughout the twentieth century and since. This is not just because they are orthodoxies and all orthodoxy must be challengeable, but because orthodoxy stymies generative art practice and thought about art. Unexamined clichés about the past and imagined power structures in the present define the types of art that are produced. At present, therefore, most artworld practice and discourse offers little that subverts a replication of the mechanisms and values of power. Instead we embody and replicate its mechanisms. While the commercial part of the artworld will have no problem with that fact, there are many artworld practitioners – including many of those on the biennial circuit, many funded through public subsidy or charitable donation and the self-funded – who claim a desire for something else for their art. Art, understood specifically as generative within disciplinary lines, has the potential to create new, nuanced and more complex stories and these may also instantiate more complex selves and more complex societies. The idea of disciplinarity is an anathema to many in the artworld, particularly to those who favour the egalitarian (and hypocritical) idea that anyone is an artist and anything can be art. The existence of artworld orthodoxy indicates the presence, despite the artworld claiming otherwise, of its institutionalisation and therefore its disciplinarity. There are no orthodoxies without institutions. It is not only the monied end of the artworld that is institutional but all participants collectively define and perform the Institutional definition of art. All participate within the orthodoxies presented as inevitable. G. E. R. Lloyd demonstrated that all disciplines operate in a tension between orthodoxy and innovation, creating and policing norms and values that change over time. If we understand Foucault and the operation of power, we understand that to imagine ourselves in a space outside the mechanisms of power, including artworld power, is to imagine a utopia; that is, literally, a space that exists nowhere. I have argued that when we do imagine we are outside power's mechanisms, or when we imagine that we operate in a binary model of power, we can only fail to address power as it actually operates and, further, we are likely to reproduce unwittingly its exclusions and excesses by virtue of denying our hand in its processes.

Looking at the artworld specifically, our desire, our self-interest is defined institutionally. Discourse determines our desires, our self-interest. This was described in the shift that occurred at the turn of the millennium when, for the first time in over a decade, the artworld embraced the political, the ethical, the socially engaged. This book is an attempt at redefining our self-interest in terms of an open disciplinarity, not only so that we acknowledge how we do in fact operate, but so that we can define for ourselves our values in ways that are distinct from neoliberalism. As with other knowledge-forming disciplines, this process of self-definition does not render immune an individual practitioner or the discipline as a whole from also taking on wider totalising discourse, including neoliberalism. Just as some 'good' (in endogenous terms) philosophy served Nazism (Heidegger, Nietzsche), some good philosophy served the resistance (Sartre, Arendt) and today some good (in endogenous terms) anthropology directly serves the market and the US military, whereas other good anthropology serves a politics of resistance against neoliberal globalisation. What endogenous disciplinary values afford is a *negotiation* with other values and mechanisms, including neoliberalism, from a disciplinary-specific point of view, not a total immunity from other pressures, knowledges, beliefs, desires. Because the artworld has surrendered the authority to judge what comprises good art, to judge what we do in disciplinary-specific terms, both the market and neoliberalism have stepped into the vacuum that we have created. We have no way of articulating our own value and values except through aping other disciplines or praxes, or through neoliberal terms.

To view art as a discipline akin to other knowledge-forming disciplines is a strategic move. As the institutional definition of art describes, it can be demonstrated that the artworld indeed *disciplines* both practice and discourse through a process of normative inclusion and exclusion. Nevertheless, the artworld is yet to acknowledge openly that art is a knowledge-forming discipline, hence the artworld loses what is positive and generative about knowledge-forming disciplines. Other knowledge-forming disciplines aim at new disciplinary knowledge that is more nuanced or more complex, and, occasionally, paradigm shifts occur which are understood as truer or more accurate than previous ones. Art can be understood in these terms. If the artworld chooses to understand art as a type of knowing, then our collective energies may be directed in art-specific generative directions which are beneficial for the discipline of art overall, in that mediocrity and cliché are not prized but avoided. Many instances of contemporary art proffer cliché and unexamined orthodoxy, thereby serving to prop up the status quo, and many things glossed as art are nothing other than commodities or instances of social amelioration. More importantly perhaps, creating art in terms of discipline-specific excellence would also be beneficial for society because the nuance and complexity that would be engendered inherently undermines totalising discourse, offering values that are distinct from those of the market or the state.

Further, art in itself offers something distinct from other disciplines which similarly produce complexity, nuance and values in addition to neoliberalism. Art is a praxis discipline but unlike other praxes, such as education and psychotherapy which have specific aims including learning and health, art is aimless. This aimlessness plays a vital role in society. Aimless generativity embodies and enacts the importance of the individual, performing the role as differentiated other, in a society comprised of differentiated others. Art plays a vital role in society in both its storytelling role when these stories are various, complex and nuanced, and as constitutive of the public realm.

Art is vital to a society that values freedom, equality, diversity, plurality (and is even more vital in those that do not). Endemic values that have been constant to art practice throughout modernity are individual agency, autonomy, creation of the self, freedom, plurality. These values are political in a modern era defined by shifts in power and money. Because art is an authored action in public, and because of its endemic values, which are also the very values of modernity, art in the modern era embodies, enacts or negotiates these values as no other discipline or praxis does. For as long as there are totalising discourses that deny or undermine these values endemic to art specifically, art will continue to have a vital role.

Art fulfils this role, resists totalising discourse and mechanisms, only when its full diversity is supported through discourse enacted through a variety of supporting institutional mechanisms. Institutional here is to be understood as the institution of the artworld as a whole as described by the Institutional definition of art and not any single or group of formal organisations. This book is an attempt at creating new institutional discourses for contemporary art practice that value and support this plurality. Plurality is not the endless variation on a basic matrix, which exists in both the market and the biennial circuit and currently feels normal and even plural, but the kind of plurality that is almost unimaginable until it exists.

According to Hannah Arendt, a political theorist whose most important writing was done immediately after the Second World War, storytelling is central to society, to action and to politics. Art is the enactment of plurality that undermines the totalitarian grid (be it the Nazi and fascist ones of her own times, or the neoliberal one of ours). When art enacts its potential to express collectively plurality, as distinct from the endless variation of a single or few matrices, it becomes inherently politically potent. The vital role of art in society does not lie simply in the amelioration of social ills or illustrating oppression, as Rancière points out. The public realm is a space for the establishment of our public identities, for the recognition of a common reality, and for the assessment of the actions of others.[7] Unlike other knowledge-forming disciplines, art does something more than invent new, nuanced or more complex stories: it enacts the plurality inherent in this process and, in so doing, challenges orthodoxy. Art also constitutes the public realm. Art is action in public. Arendt writes:

> [action] is the only activity that goes on directly between men without the intermediary of things or matter, corresponds to the human condition of plurality … this plurality is specifically *the* condition – not only the *conditio sine qua non*, but the *conditio per quam* – of all political life.[8]

Plurality is not only indispensable to politics but plurality is the necessary condition that makes politics possible. In connecting action, storytelling and plurality as the very basis for the political, Hannah Arendt gives artists concerned with the social realm another way of considering our practice. Art enacts plurality, diversity, the alterity that baffles simple categorisation and hierarchies and, by doing so in public, art is exquisitely constitutive of the public realm. At times, art creates radical new stories that profoundly alter our way of seeing, disrupting the order of things, making new sense of our place and time in ways that undermine totalising discourse. Sometimes art's storytelling is profoundly revolutionary in its evocation and enactment of *something else.*

Notes

Introduction

1. My BA in fine art practice was at Victoria College, Prahran, Melbourne, Australia in the Painting Department. Due to a quirk of the education system at the time, when my college was being merged with Melbourne University, it became possible to take modules at the university as well. Consequently, I took modules in Philosophy and History, and Philosophy of Science, as well as Art History in years one and two instead of other practice-based modules such as sculpture and printmaking. A few years later, my MA was entirely academic (or theoretical, to distinguish it from practice-based) in 'Gender, Society, Culture' at Birkbeck College, University of London. Ten years later I began a 50:50 practice:academic PhD at Oxford Brookes University, which allowed me the opportunity to undertake original research in both academic-theoretical and practical arenas, exploring 'Art as a Democratic Act: the interplay of content and context in contemporary art'.
2. There is a tiny fraction of the artworld who might be called global practitioners. These are the artists and curators who jet about the world, regularly exhibiting art in disparate locations and who have three or more geographical bases for their practice. Nevertheless, these artists and curators also have cultural backgrounds which inform their perception and expectations of the art and culture around them. They are also local.
3. Michel de Certeau, *The Practice of Everyday Life*, trans. Steven Rendall (Berkeley: University of California Press, 1984).
4. Grant H. Kester, *Conversation Pieces: Community and Communication in Modern Art* (Berkeley, CA and London: University of California Press, 2004); Gregory Sholette, *Dark Matter: Art and Politics in the Age of Enterprise Culture* (New York and London: Pluto Press, 2011); Nato

Thompson and Gregory Sholette, eds., *The Interventionists: Users' Manual for the Creative Disruption of Everyday Life* (Cambridge, MA and, London: The MIT Press, 2004); James Putnam, *Art and Artifact: The Museum as Medium* (London: Thames & Hudson, 2009.

5. Pierre Bourdieu, *Distinction: A Social Critique of the Judgement of Taste,* trans. Richard Nice (Cambridge, MA: Harvard University Press, 1984).

Chapter 1

1. Robert Hughes, 'The Rise of Andy Warhol', in Brian Wallis, ed., *Art After Modernism: Rethinking Representation* (New York and Boston: New Museum of Contemporary Art, 1984), pp. 45–57. Reprinted from *The New York Review of Books,* 18 February 1982, pp. 6–10.
2. David Harvey, *A Brief History of Neoliberalism* (Oxford: Oxford University Press, 2005).
3. Joseph Stiglitz, *Globalisation and its Discontents* (London: Penguin, 2002).
4. Paul Langley, *World Financial Orders: An Historical International Political Economy* (London and New York: Routledge, 2002), p. 110.
5. The beginning of a generalised market orientation within the London artworld began with the market successes of the YBAs (Young British Artists) in the early 1990s but the all-pervasiveness across the London artworld of neoliberal norms and values took a little more time. It has been argued by Claire Bishop, among others, that the shift occurred in the wake of the fall of the Berlin wall and the crisis in the left that this engendered. This may also be a factor but I argue that we must understand the impact of simultaneous economic structural changes that occurred at that time, namely neoliberalism.
6. Personal interview with Michael Dixon, Director of Natural History Museum, and Frances Windsor, Policy Advisor to the Director, 16 November 2006.
7. Mary Warnock and Mark Wallinger, eds., *Art For All: Their Policies and Our Culture* (London: Peer, 2000).
8. Lars Nittve, 'Foreword', in Iwona Blazwick, ed., *Century City: Art and Culture in the Modern Metropolis,* exhibition catalogue (London: Tate Publishing, 2001).
9. The critical reception of 'Century City' was ambivalent at best. This may have been the product of a right-wing press hostile to the opening up of such an important institutional space to the art of non-white

people and non-traditional cultural centres without due regard to traditional ideas in art history. Eleanor Heartney's 'Boomtowns of the Avant-Garde – Tate Modern Exhibition Critical Essay', is one example of the more balanced reviews (*Art in America*, 89 (9) (September 2001), p. 65).

10. Three Year Funding Agreement 2003–2006 between the Board of Trustees of the Tate Gallery and the Department for Culture, Media and Sport.

11. Information about exhibition audience figures is readily available through Freedom of Information request. For my doctoral thesis, I crunched the numbers to come up with the surprising correlation between corporate sponsorship and higher audience figures, speculating that this was not only due to increased marketing budgets as part of the sponsorship deal but also because there tended to be greater numbers of press releases from Tate when an exhibition was sponsored. I concluded that, all things considered, the exhibition's subject – the artist him- or herself – had little effect on audience figures.

12. Concurrent with the rise in neoliberalism, the location of the avant-garde shifted from outside to inside the commercial sector. Infrastructure changes can be shown in the post-war period: from the 1950s to 1970s the avant-garde was located in artist-run studios and initiatives, with two 'independent' gallery exceptions, the ICA and the Beaux Arts Gallery (1923–65). From the 1980s to mid-1990s the avant-garde was found largely within publicly funded independent galleries in the East End of London such as Matt's or Chisenhale, or other artist initiatives.

13. Though not as triumphalist and crass as is often interpreted, Fukuyama, following Hegel, refers specifically to the end of history as dialectic, but despite this nod towards Marxist thought he does see the historical dialectic as rightfully resolved in favour of liberal capitalist democracy.

14. Peter Bürger, *Theory of the Avant-Garde*, trans. Michael Shaw (Manchester: Manchester University Press, 1984 [1974]).

15. Gregory Sholette, *Dark Matter: Art and Politics in the Age of Enterprise Culture* (New York and London: Pluto Press, 2011).

16. Louisa Buck, *Market Matters: The Dynamics of the Contemporary Art Market* (London: Arts Council England, 2004), p. 6.

17. John Holden, *Publicly Funded Culture and the Creative Industries* (London: Demos, Arts Council England, June 2007).

18. Olav Velthuis, *Talking Prices: Symbolic Meanings of Prices on the Market for Contemporary Art* (Princeton, NJ and Oxford: Princeton University Press, 2005).

19. Ibid.
20. Ibid., p. 86.
21. Ibid., p. 82, citing Stuart Plattner, *High Art Down Home: An Economic Ethnography of a Local Art Market* (Chicago: University of Chicago Press, 1996), p. 195.
22. Pascal Gielen, *The Murmuring of the Artistic Multitude: Global Art, Memory and Post-Fordism* (Amsterdam: Valiz, 2009), especially pp. 135–89.
23. Ibid., p. 161.
24. Ibid., p. 180.
25. Ibid., p. 178.
26. Ibid., p. 160.
27. Jean Gadrey, *New Economy, New Myth* (New York and London: Routledge, 2001), p. 84.
28. Ibid., p. 82.
29. Ibid., p. 83.
30. Discussed by Tracey Emin and Oliver Baker, Sotheby's Head of Contemporary Art, who explains the disparity with: 'the short answer is yes there has been a sort of prejudice'. *What Price Art?* part of *ArtShock* series, Channel 4, 15 March 2006.
31. Jonathan Nitzan and Shimshon Bichler, *The Global Political Economy of Israel* (London: Pluto Press, 2002).
32. Michel Callon, ed., 'Introduction', in *The Laws of the Markets* (Oxford: Blackwell, 1998), p. 49.
33. Ibid., p. 44.
34. Jean Gadrey, *New Economy, New Myth*, pp. 78–82.
35. Callon, 'Introduction', in *The Laws of the Markets*, p. 48.
36. Andrew Brighton, 'Towards a Command Culture: New Labour's Cultural Policy and Soviet Socialist Realism', in Mary Warnock and Mark Wallinger, eds., *Art for All*, p. 40; Munira Mirza, 'Introduction', in Munira Mirza *et al.*, *Culture Vultures: Is UK Arts Policy Damaging the Arts?* (London: Policy Exchange, 2006).
37. Spanning 1986–1994, the Uruguay round was the eighth round of Multilateral Trade Negotiations (MTN) conducted within the framework of the General Agreement on Tariffs and Trade (GATT). The round transformed GATT into the World Trade Organization (WTO).
38. The Corner House, *Briefing Paper 32: Political Organising Behind TRIPS* (Sturminster Newton, Dorset: September 2004).
39. David Bainbridge, *Software Copyright Law*, 4th edn (London: Butterworths, 1999).

40. Andreas Rahmatian, *Copyright and Creativity: The Making of Property Rights in Creative Works* (Cheltenham, UK and Northampton, MA, US: Edward Elgar, 2011).
41. Jaime Stapleton, 'Art Intellectual Property and the Knowledge Economy', unpublished doctoral thesis (2002), pp. 23–44.
42. With literary works, which include fine art, it is not the idea conveyed by an artwork that is protected by copyright law but the form in which it is recorded or is manifested. It is notable that there is a different emphasis in copyright law between the continental tradition as *droit d'auteur* and the Anglo tradition of ownership. The point I am making here is about the trade and monetisation of intellectual property, both aspects of knowledge economy innovation. For a critique of the marketplace for ideas, see 'Against Intellectual Property' by Brian Martin, first published in *Philosophy and Social Action,* 21 (3) (1995), and for an economist's view, see Elad Harrison, *Intellectual Property Rights, Innovation and Software Technologies: The Economics of Monopoly Rights and Knowledge Disclosure* (Cheltenham: Edward Elgar, 2008).
43. Bowie Bonds were an asset-backed security. The asset at the core of the investment was the current and future revenues generated from David Bowie's first 25 albums. Issued in 1997, the ten-year bonds were bought for US $55 million by the Prudential Insurance Company of America.
44. Lucy Lippard, *Six Years: The Dematerialization of the Art Object from 1966 to 1972...* (Berkeley and London: University of California Press, 1997).
45. The Shanghai biennial began in 1994 but in 2000 changed to accept international submissions
46. Compiled by Dr Iain Robertson, Head of Art Business Studies, Sotheby's Institute of Art, for the Tate Modern conference 'Good Business makes the Best Art' on 10 October 2009.
47. Clement Greenberg, who I discuss in more detail in Chapter 4, is one of many who may be understood as occupying an elitist and Eurocentric position, typical of early and mid-twentieth-century Anglo-American philosophy and art history.
48. Nancy Jachec, *Politics and Painting at the Venice Biennale, 1948–64: Italy and the Idea of Europe* (Manchester: Manchester University Press, 2007).
49. Luc Boltanski and Ève Chiapello, *The New Spirit of Capitalism,* trans. Gregory Elliot (London: Verso, 2005 [1999]).

50. Michael Sandel, 'Reith lecture: a price for everything but at what cost?' *Times Online*, 13 June 2009. Available online. <http://entertainment.timesonline.co.uk/tol/arts_and_entertainment/tv_and_radio/article 6485444.ece> Accessed 9 July 2011. *The Times* (London, England), ISSN 0140-0460, 13 June 2009, p. 4.

Chapter 2

1. The disastrous legacy of Greenberg's writing for analytic philosophy in a postmodern artworld has been noted by Diarmuid Costello, a philosopher straddling the continental/analytic divide. Diarmuid Costello, 'Greenberg's Kant and the Fate of Aesthetics in Contemporary Art Theory', *The Journal of Aesthetics and Art Criticism*, 65 (2) (Spring 2007).
2. Gerald Raunig, *Art and Revolution: Transversal Activism in the Long Twentieth Century*, trans. Aileen Derieg (Los Angeles: Semiotexte, 2007), p. 16. 'The spread of art to the streets, to the masses, into life, slogans like "everyone is an artist", "art for everyone" and "from everyone", transgressing the boundaries of art into the social field and the political field – none of these are the invention of the avant-garde of the 20th century, of Beuys' generation or of the cultural policies of the 1970s, but they are instead, so to speak trans-historical patterns of art practice and politics: Tragedies would become celebrations of humanity, asserts Wagner, education in a free society much become a purely artistic education, "... and every man will become in some respect truly an artist".'
3. Morris Weitz, 'The Role of Theory in Aesthetics', in Francis J. Coleman, ed., *Contemporary Studies in Aesthetics* (New York: McGraw-Hill, 1968), pp. 84–94.
4. Ludwig Wittgenstein, *Philosophical Investigations*, trans. G. E. M. Anscombe, ed., 2nd edn (Oxford: Blackwell, 1958), Part I, sections 65–75. Wittgenstein wrote little directly about art or aesthetics. See Malcolm Budd on this in 'Wittgenstein on Aesthetics', in *Aesthetic Essays* (Oxford: Oxford University Press, 2008), pp. 252–77.
5. Arthur Danto, 'The Artworld', *Journal of Philosophy*, 61 (19), pp. 571–84; p. 573.
6. Ibid., p. 581.
7. One later example is Paul Mattick's *Art in its Time: Theories and Practices of Modern Aesthetics* (London: Routledge, 2003). Ironically or otherwise, he comes from a broadly Marxist perspective in his criticism.

8. Michael C. Fitzgerald, *Making Modernism: Picasso and the Creation of the Market for Twentieth-Century Art* (Berkeley, CA and London: University of California Press, 1996).
9. Philosopher Dabney Townsend writes about this 'democratic engagement' in favourable terms, claiming that art has a new relationship with its audience and that together artist and audience have produced a new type of aesthetics, the product of postmodern subjectivities. Here I argue to the contrary, that changes in artworld discourse towards populism must be understood as an artworld engagement with neoliberal norms and values and not the postmodern engagement or democratised relationship with audience that Townsend describes. Dabney Townsend, *An Introduction to Aesthetics* (Malden, MA and Oxford: Blackwell, 1997).
10. Claire Bishop, *Artificial Hells: Participatory Art and the Politics of Spectatorship* (London: Verso 2012) p. 202.
11. Bruno Latour and Steve Woolgar, *Laboratory Life: The Social Construction of Scientific Facts* (London: Sage Publications, 1979).
12. Liz Ellis, 'Do You Want to Be in My Gang: An Account of Ethics and Aesthetics in Contemporary Art Practice', *n.paradoxa*, 2 (1997), pp. 6–14.
13. Gail Day, *Dialectical Passions: Negation in Postwar Art Theory* (New York and Chichester: Columbia University Press, 2011), p. 23.
14. Thomas Hirschhorn and a few other contemporary artists participated in this exhibition, and although Hirschhorn, for example, regards his work as radical or political, the bridge he built in signature brown packaging tape from the gallery's cafe to the long-established anarchist bookshop on the other side of the alley was more an exercise in Hirschhorn branding than any type of political or radical act.
15. Mark Sladen, Protest & Survive review, *frieze* magazine, 57 (March 2001).
16. Gail Day, *Dialectical Passions*, p. 23.
17. David Willer, ed., *Network Exchange Theory* (Westport, CT: Praeger, 1999), p. 4.
18. One example from personal experience was the exhibition 'empire and I' that I curated. I invited eight other artists from a range of backgrounds to explore the legacy of the British colonial project: Niema Khan, Eamon O'Kane, Tertia Longmire, Erika Tan, Anthony Key, Shaheen Merali, Lorrice Douglas, Rea. It was eventually shown in 1999 at Pitzhanger Manor and Gallery, then at an arts centre in Cheltenham. I began working on the exhibition in 1995 and was told by most museum

curators and directors at the time, including Iniva (the International Institute for Visual Arts) that postcolonialism had already been explored and there was no need for another exhibition on the subject, even if this one for the first time included the art of white British and other white artists with artists of Chinese origin alongside indigenous, Asian and Black artists.

19. George Dickie, *Art Circle: A Theory of Art* (Chicago: Spectrum Press, 1997), pp. 80–2.

20. Available online. <www.tate.org.uk/britain/exhibitions/intelligence/deller.htm> Accessed 20 June 2005.

21. Jacques Rancière, *Dissensus: On Politics and Aesthetics*, trans. and ed. Steven Corcoran, ed. (London and New York: Continuum, 2010).

22. Philosopher Derek Matravers has commented on this interpretation of Dickie, nuancing it. Matravers points out that 'when Dickie says that an artist has "to participate with understanding" this amounts to putting forward objects to the public within a context of appreciation and reasons for appreciation. Think of the analogy with knighthood. A knight is someone dubbed on the shoulder by the Queen. However, that is only half the story. She does not dub just anyone on the shoulder; she does so in the context of a set of reasons and only people who "fit" those reasons are made knights. *However*, one of the reasons for something being art in the contemporary artword is (weirdly) being "dubbed" art by someone who is a recognised artist. It would be as if being dubbed on the shoulder by the Queen was *itself a reason* to be dubbed on the shoulder by the Queen (which is doubtfully coherent). So I would say that Dickie's theory allows that "anything the artworld says is art is art" because it *allows* a plethora of reasons in. But it does not *entail* it.'

23. Robert Yanal, 'The Institutional Theory of Art', vol. 2, pp. 508–12, in Michael Kelly, ed., *Encyclopedia of Aesthetics*, 4 vols (Oxford: Oxford University Press, 1998), p. 510.

24. Julian Stallabrass, *Art Incorporated: The Story of Contemporary Art* (Oxford: Oxford University Press, 2004), especially 'New World Order', pp. 29–72.

25. 'Martha Rosler interviewed by Robert Fichter and Paul Rutkovsy', in Glenn Harper, ed., *Interventions and Provocation: Conversations on Art, Culture and Resistance* (Albany: State University of New York Press, 1998), p. 13.

26. The story is admittedly more complicated than this. See Jack Bankowsky, Alison M. Gingeras and Catherine Wood, eds., *Pop Life: Art in a Material World* (London: Tate Publishing, 2009).

27. Philosopher of History, R.G. Collingwood argues this point, adding that it is possible to reflect history accurately when the historian is aware of this autobiographical tendency. R. G. Collingwood, *The Idea of History* (Oxford: Oxford University Press, 1994 [1936]).
28. David Smith, 'He's our favourite artist. So why do the galleries hate him so much?', *The Observer*, Sunday 11 January 2004; Ruaridh Nicoll, 'The frame game: Why should our galleries' curators be bullied in their choice of art?', *The Observer*, Sunday 28 March 2004.
29. Pascal Gielen, *The Murmuring of the Artistic Multitude: Global Art, Memory and Post-Fordism* (Amsterdam: Valiz, 2009), pp. 17–68 and 18–45.
30. Pierre Bourdieu, *Distinction: A Social Critique of the Judgement of Taste*, trans. Richard Nice (London: Routledge & Kegan Paul, 1984).
31. Oskar Bätschmann, *The Artist in the Modern World: The Conflict Between Market and Self-Expression* (New Haven: Yale, and Cologne: Dumont, 1997).

Chapter 3

1. Oskar Bätschmann, *The Artist in the Modern World.*
2. Gail Day, *Dialectical Passions*, p. 6.
3. Tony Bennett, *Culture: A Reformer's Science* (London and Thousand Oaks, CA: Sage Publications, 1998).
4. Antonio Gramsci, *Selections from The Prison Notebooks of Antonio Gramsci*, trans. and ed. Q. Hoare and G. Nowell Smith, eds. (London: Laurence & Wishart, 1971), pp. 265–6.
5. Neil Barnett, 'Including Ourselves: New Labour and Engagement with Public Services', *Management Decision*, 40 (4) (2002), pp. 310–17.
6. Anthony Giddens, *The Third Way: The Renewal of Social Democracy* (Cambridge: Polity, 1998).
7. Alex Callinicos, *Against the Third Way: An Anti-Capitalist Critique* (Cambridge: Polity, 2001), p. 103.
8. Ibid., p. 62.
9. Chin-tao Wu, *Privatising Culture: Corporate Art Intervention since the 1980s* (London and New York: Verso, 2002).
10. Luther H. Martin, Huck Gutman and Patrick H. Hutton, eds., *Technologies of the Self: A Seminar With Michel Foucault* (London: Tavistock, 1988), pp. 18–19.
11. See Jacques Rancière, *Dissensus*, pp. 136–7.
12. Ibid., p. 142.

13. For example, see *Do It Yourself: A Handbook for Changing our World*, edited by the Trapese Collective (Pluto Press, 2007).
14. Paolo Freire, *Pedagogy of the Oppressed*, trans. Myra Bergman Ramos (New York: Herder and Herder, 1972), p. 95.
15. Chantal Mouffe, *The Return of the Political* (London: Verso, 1993 [1997]), pp. 18–21.
16. Collingwood, *The Idea of History*.
17. Alex Callinicos, *Against the Third Way*, p. 37.
18. Ibid., p. 113.
19. Michel Foucault, *History of Sexuality*, vol 1: *An Introduction*, trans. Robert Hurley (Harmondsworth: Penguin, 1981 [1978]), p. 96.
20. Jean-Paul Sartre, *Being and Nothingness: An Essay on Phenomenological Ontology*, trans. Hazel E. Barnes (1957) (London: Methuen & Co Ltd, 1966 [1943]), pp. 555–6.
21. Michel Foucault, 'On the Genealogy of Ethics', in Paul Rabinow, ed., *The Foucault Reader* (Harmondsworth: Penguin, 1986) p. 351.
22. Michel Foucault, 'The Subject and Power', *Critical Inquiry*, 8 (4) (Summer, 1982), p. 785.
23. Kevin Craig Boileau, *Genuine Reciprocity and Group Authenticity: Foucault's Developments on Sartre's Social Ontology* (Lanham, New York and Oxford: University Press of America, 2000), p. 133.
24. Ibid., pp. 125–39.
25. Michel Foucault, 'The Subject and Power' cited in Kevin Craig Boileau, ibid., p. 134.
26. Michel Foucault, *Politics, Philosophy, Culture: Interviews and Other Writings, 1977–1984*, trans. Alan Sheridan (New York and London: Routledge, 1988), p. 155.
27. Michel Foucault, *History of Sexuality*, vol. 1, p. 96.
28. Gerald Raunig, *Art and Revolution*, p. 46.
29. Martin *et al.*, *Technologies of the Self: A Seminar With Michel Foucault*, pp. 18–19.
30. Nicholas Thomas, *Entangled Objects: Exchange, Material Culture, and Colonialism in the Pacific* (Cambridge, MA and London: Harvard University Press, 1991).
31. Ibid., pp. 123–5.
32. Donna Haraway, *Primate Visions: Gender, Race and Nature in the World of Modern Science* (London: Verso, 1992 [1989]), pp. 26–58.
33. Serge Guilbaut, *How New York Stole the Idea of Modern Art: Abstract Expressionism, Freedom, and the Cold War*, trans. Arthur Goldhammer (Chicago and London: University of Chicago Press, 1983); Nancy Jachec,

The Philosophy and Politics of Abstract Expressionism, 1940–1960 (Cambridge and New York: Cambridge University Press, 2000).

34. Michel Foucault, 'Intellectuals and Power', reprinted from *L'Arc*, 49 (1972), pp. 3–10, in Buchard, ed., *Language, Counter-Memory, Practice*, pp. 205–17, p. 214.

35. Iain McLean, *Rational Choice and British Politics: An Analysis of Rhetoric and Manipulation from Peel to Blair* (Oxford: Oxford University Press, 2001).

Chapter 4

1. 'Kant's theory was processed by Clive Bell, whose 1914 book, *Art*, portions of which still appear in nearly all introductory anthologies, is a virtual Kant-made-simple, and whose central concept of "significant form" strip Kantian aesthetic judgement of anything except a preoccupation with design and composition', Robert J. Yanal, 'Kant on Aesthetic Ideas and Beauty' in Robert J. Yanal, ed., *Institutions of Art: Reconsiderations of George Dickie's Philosophy* (Pennsylvania State University Press, 1994), pp. 157–83.

2. Oskar Bätschmann, *The Artist in the Modern World*, pp. 74–5. Also see Nietzsche, *Twilight of the Idols: and, The Anti-Christ*, trans. R. J. Hollingdale (Harmondsworth: Penguin, 1968).

3. Allan Kaprow, *Essays on the Blurring of Life and Art* (Berkeley: University of California Press, 1993), p. 201.

4. Lucy Lippard, *Six Years: The Dematerialization of the Art Object from 1966 to 1972.*

5. T. J. Clark, *Farewell to an Idea: Episodes from a History of Modernism* (New Haven and London: Yale University Press, 1999). Interestingly, Clark connects Modernism with socialism.

6. Greenberg's famous essay 'Art and Kitsch' (1939) occupies a more complex position than this one-sentence summary implies. Greenberg is in fact hostile to the market for its support of kitsch: 'Because it can be turned out mechanically, kitsch has become an integral part of our productive system in a way in which true culture could never be, except accidentally. It has been capitalized at a tremendous investment which must show commensurate returns; it is compelled to extend as well as to keep its markets.' For Greenberg, the market is bourgeois whereas the true inheritors of the avant-garde should be the ruling class; a responsibility they have shirked, in his opinion.

7. Diarmuid Costello, 'Greenberg, Kant and the Fate of Aesthetics in Contemporary Art Theory', *The Journal of Aesthetics and Art Criticism*, 65 (2) (Spring 2007), p. 218.
8. Clement Greenberg, 'Autonomies of Art' lecture, Moral Philosophy and Art Symposium, Mountain Lake, Virginia, October 1980. Available online. <www.sharecom.ca/greenberg/autonomies.html> Accessed 25 October 2012. A good illustration of the issues that arose historically within the formalist debate can be seen in the exchange between Greenberg and Max Kosloff aired in *Artforum* over November and December 1967, collected in John O'Brian, ed., *Clement Greenberg: The Collected Essays and Criticism*, vol. 4: *Modernism with a Vengeance* (Chicago and London: University of Chicago Press, 1993), pp. 272–6.
9. This is the stereotypical position. Greenberg actually argues against the idea of the inherent superiority of abstract art in, 'The Case for Abstract Art', *Clement Greenberg: The Collected Essays and Criticism*, vol. 4: *Modernism with a Vengeance*, pp. 75–84.
10. Adolfo Sánchez Vázquez, *Art and Society: Essays in Marxist Aesthetics*, trans. Mario Riofrancos (1965) (New York: Monthly Review Press, 1973), p. 84.
11. Immanuel Kant, 'Groundwork of the Metaphysics of Morals', pp. 37–108, in *Practical Philosophy*, trans. Mary Gregor (Cambridge: Cambridge University Press, 1995), 4:435, p. 85.
12. Jan Verwoert, 'Control I'm here: A call for the free use of the means of producing communication, in curating and in general', in Paul O'Neill and Mick Wilson, eds., *Curating and the Educational Turn* (Amsterdam: Open Editions / de Appel, 2010), p. 30.
13. The beginning of the Modern era is much debated in academic circles. For literary critics, the early Modern period in England begins with the Elizabethans. Like any epoch, not only is modernity both a construct and veracious, but it has origins and manifestations that are different in different parts of the world.
14. Oskar Bätschmann, *The Artist in the Modern World.*
15. Clement Greenberg, 'Art and Kitsch' (1939,) in *Art and Culture: Critical Essays* (Boston: Beacon Press, 1965 [1961]).
16. In addition to Bätschmann, see T. J. Clark, *The Painting of Modern Life: Paris in the Art of Manet and his Followers* (London: Thames and Hudson, 1985).
17. Claire Bishop, ed., *Participation* (London: Whitechapel, 2006), p. 12. The binary that Bishop explores in *Participation* is the author–collective binary, which forms part of the discourse around lifelike art.

In Chapter 6, I quote Hannah Arendt who is highly critical of the idea of an authorless action. Though I don't focus on this aspect, the assumptions within the author–collectives binary can be understood within my critique of the assumptions within lifelike art.

18. Lucy Lippard, *Six Years: The Dematerialization of the Art Object from 1966 to 1972*, p. 263.

19. Rachel Schreiber, 'Net.art: Shedding the Utopian Moment?', *Link: A Critical Journal on the Arts in Baltimore and the World*, 7 (2001). Also see Martha Rosler, 'Shedding the Utopian Moment' (1985), in *Illuminating Video: An Essential Guide to Video Art*, ed. Doug Hall and Sally Jo Fifer ([New York?]: Aperture in association with the Bay Area Video Coalition c.1990)

20. With a generalised 'conceptualism' informing most contemporary art practices, painting has come to be practised and understood within the lifelike tradition, at least when it directly addresses social and political concerns such as the environment. In some sense, the once robust demarcation is less trenchantly defended. Nevertheless, painting's long association with commodification and the market is born out in the league tables for contemporary art, which are topped by painters mostly and sculptors.

21. Johanna Drucker, *Sweet Dreams: Contemporary Art and Complicity* (Chicago and London: University of Chicago Press, 2005).

22. Claire Bishop, 'The Social Turn: Collaboration and its Discontents', *Artforum*, 44 (6) (February 2006), pp. 178–83; Grant H. Kester, 'Another Turn', *Artforum*, 44 (9) (May 2006), p. 22; Claire Bishop, 'Responds', *Artforum*, 44 (9) (May 2006), p. 24.

23. Benjamin Buchloh, *Neo Avant-Garde and Culture Industry: Essays on European and American Art from 1955–1975* (Cambridge, MA: MIT Press, 2000), pp. xxxi–xxxiii.

24. Oskar Bätschmann, *The Artist in the Modern World*, pp. 52–76.

25. Andrew Brighton, 'Towards a Command Culture: New Labour's Cultural Policy and Soviet Socialist Realism', in Mary Warnock and Mark Wallinger, eds., *Art for All*, pp. 36–41.

26. Neil Barnett, 'Including Ourselves: New Labour and Engagement with Public Services', *Management Decision*, 40 (4) (2002), pp. 310–17. References cited include T. Fitzpatrick, 'The Rise of Market Collectivism', *Social Policy Review*, 10 (1999) and D. Hodgson, '"Empowering Customers Through Education" or Governing Without Government?', in A. Sturdy, I. Grugulis and H. Willmott, eds., *Customer Service Empowerment and Entrapment* (Basingstoke: Palgrave, 2001).

27. See, for example, the arguments made by Alan Bowness, former director of Tate Gallery, in *The Conditions of Success: How the Modern Artist Rises to Fame* (London: Thames & Hudson, 1989).
28. Munira Mirza, 'Introduction', and Sara Selwood, 'Unreliable Evidence: The Rhetorics of Data Collection in the Cultural Sector', in Munira Mirza, ed., *Culture Vultures*, p. 42.
29. Oskar Bätschmann, *The Artist in the Modern World*, pp. 44–52.
30. 'From Criticism to Complicity' (1986), in Charles Harrison and Paul Wood, eds., *Art in Theory, 1900–1990: An Anthology of Changing Ideas* (Malden, MA: Blackwell, 1992), pp. 1080–4.
31. Oskar Bätschmann, *The Artist in the Modern World*, citing James Barry, *An Account of a Series of Pictures in the Great Room of the Society of Arts, Manufactures and Commerce at the Adelphi* (London: T. Cadell and J. Walter, 1783), pp. 7–21.
32. Michel Callon, *The Laws of the Markets*.
33. Paolo Virno, *A Grammar of the Multitude: For an Analysis of Contemporary Forms of Life*, trans. Isabella Bertoletti, James Cascaito and Andrea Casson (Los Angeles, CA: Semiotext(e), 2004); Michael Hardt and Antonio Negri, *Empire* (Cambridge, MA and London: Harvard University Press, 2000); Michael Hardt and Antonio Negri, *Multitude: War and Democracy in the Age of Empire* (London: Penguin, 2006).
34. Olav Velthuis, *Talking Prices*.

Chapter 5

1. A few examples amongst many include Arjo Klamer, ed., *The Value of Culture: On the Relationship Between Economics and the Arts* (Amsterdam: Amsterdam University Press, 1996); 'The Rise of the Art Market' conference, Tate Britain, 2007; 'Good Business Makes the Best Art' conference, Tate Modern, 2009; 'Rules of the Game: Value and Money', a series of talks at August Art Gallery, London, 2011.
2. Jean-François Lyotard, *The Postmodern Condition: A Report on Knowledge*, trans. Geoff Bennington and Brian Massumi (Manchester: Manchester University Press, 1987), p. 76.
3. Using the term contra-power is to evoke Antonio Negri's use in *Subversive Spinoza: (Un) contemporary Variations*, ed. Timothy S. Murphy (Manchester: Manchester University Press, 2004).
4. See, for example, Jon Thompson, 'Art Education: from Coldstream to QAA', *Critical Quarterly*, 47 (1–2) (July 2005), p. 218; Felicity Allen, ed., *Education* (London: Whitechapel Art Gallery, MIT Press, 2011).

5. Michel Foucault, *Language, Counter-Memory, Practice: Selected Essays and Interviews*, edited by Donald F. Bouchard, trans. Donald F. Bouchard and Sherry Simon (Oxford: Basil Blackwell, 1977), pp. 207–8.
6. Bruno Latour and Steve Woolgar, *Laboratory Life: The Social Construction of Scientific Facts* (Beverly Hills and London: Sage Publications, 1979), p. 13.
7. Ibid., pp. 11–14.
8. By way of illustration, this took place at 'The Ethics of Encounter' research workshop, hosted by Stills Gallery and University of Edinburgh, Edinburgh, 3–4 March 2011.
9. For a clarification of the philosophical meaning of the word ontology, see Michael Carrithers, Matei Candea, Karen Sykes, Martin Holbraad and Soumhya Venkatesan, 'Ontology Is Just Another Word for Culture: Motion Tabled at the 2008 University of Manchester Meeting of the Group for Debates in Anthropological Theory', *Critique of Anthropology*, 30 (2010), pp. 152–200, particularly Martin Holbraad's contribution, pp. 179–85.
10. Raymond Williams, *Keywords: A Vocabulary of Culture and Society* (London: Flamingo Fontana Paperbacks, 1983 [1976]), p. 24.
11. Alfred Gell, *The Art of Anthropology: Essays and Diagrams* (New Brunswick, NJ and London: Athlone Press, 1999), p. 7.
12. Ibid., p. 3.
13. Gell also wrote on art as a social function in Alfred Gell, *Art and Agency: An Anthropological Theory* (Oxford: Clarendon, 1998).
14. Colin Renfrew, *Figuring It Out: What Are We? Where Do We Come From? The Parallel Visions of Artists and Archaeologists* (London: Thames & Hudson, 2003), p. 21.
15. Colin Renfrew, 'Art for Archaeology', in Colin Renfrew, Chris Gosden and Elizabeth DeMarrais, eds., *Substance, Memory, Display: Archaeology and Art* (Cambridge: McDonald Institute Monographs, 2004), p. 7.
16. Ibid., p. 8.
17. To distinguish the concept from the personal research that is an investigation into an established field, research here means specifically that which is produced in doctoral or professional research producing original data or syntheses.
18. One new strand in social anthropology is 'ethnographic conceptualism' proposed by social anthropologists Nikolai Ssorin-Chaikov and Olga Sosnina, with their understanding of conceptual art applied to an anthropological practice.

19. *Sweetgrass* (2009) directed by Lucien Castaing-Taylor, produced by Ilisa Barbash, shown at the Institute of Contemporary Art (ICA), London, 2011, 101 mins.
20. Colin Renfrew, *Figuring It Out*, pp. 84–90; Colin Renfrew, 'It may be Art but is it Archaeology?', in Alex Coles and Mark Dion, eds., *Mark Dion, Archaeology* (London: Black Dog Publishing), pp. 14–23.
21. John Dewey, *Art as Experience* (London: George Allen & Unwin, 1934), pp. 288–90.
22. Ibid., p. 290.
23. A term from anthropology, which resonates unfortunately with fans of science fiction. Here I mean specifically before Aboriginal Australian peoples negotiated and performed modernity, in waves through the late eighteenth, nineteenth and twentieth centuries starting from 1770, the year of Cook's 'discovery'. Aboriginal people had contact with Indonesian people for 4,000 years prior to the encounter with Europeans, and the first Europeans to arrive on Australian shores were the Dutch in 1606.
24. The traditional twentieth-century view of art shared by many historians and philosophers is articulated in R. G. Collingwood, *The Principles of Art* (Oxford: Clarendon Press, 1938).
25. Raymond Williams, *Keywords: A Vocabulary of Culture and Society* (London: Fontana, 1983 [1976]), pp. 31–3, 40–3.
26. Simon Schaffer, 'How Disciplines Look', in Georgina Born and Andrew Barry, eds., *Interdisciplinarity: Reconfiguration of the Social and Natural Sciences* (Routledge, forthcoming 2012).
27. Oskar Bätschmann, *The Artist in the Modern World.*
28. Michel Foucault, 'What is Enlightenment?', in *The Foucault Reader*, p. 42.
29. To paraphrase David Couzens Hoy's introduction to *Foucault: A Critical Reader*, p. 22.
30. G. E. R. Lloyd, *Disciplines in the Making: Cross-Cultural Perspectives on Elites, Learning and Innovation* (Oxford: Oxford University Press, 2009); G. E. R. Lloyd, *Cognitive Variations: Reflections on the Unity and Diversity of the Human Mind* (Oxford: Clarendon, 2007).
31. G. E. R. Lloyd, *Disciplines in the Making*, p. 182, referencing Thomas S. Kuhn, *The Essential Tension: Selected Studies in Scientific Tradition and Change* (Chicago: University of Chicago Press, 1977).
32. Marilyn Strathern, 'A Community of Critics? Thoughts on New Knowledge', *Journal of the Royal Anthropological Institute*, 12 (1) (2006), pp. 191–209; 'In Crisis Mode: A Comment on Interculturality', in Marilyn

Strathern, *Commons and Borderlands* (Wantage: Sean Kingston, 2004), pp. 1–14.

33. Helga Nowotny, Peter Scott and Michael Gibbons, *Re-thinking Science: Knowledge and the Public in an Age of Uncertainty* (Cambridge: Polity, 2001). The soon to be published *Interdisciplinarity: Reconfiguration of the Social and Natural Sciences,* edited by Georgina Born and Andrew Barry (Routledge) critiques this assumption, arguing instead that interdisciplines may be equally 'autonomous' and 'innovative'.

34. Georgina Born and Andrew Barry, eds., *Interdisciplinarity.* See also Andrew Barry, *Political Machines: Governing a Technological Society* (London: Athlone, 2001) and 'Pharmaceutical Matters: The Invention of Informed Materials', in *Theory, Culture and Society*, 22 (2005), pp. 51–69.

35. Ivan Illich, *Deschooling Society* (London: Calder & Boyars, 1971).

36. The main art school qualification after 1944 was the National Diploma in Design, although not all practising artists had this qualification. In 1961 the new Diploma in Art and Design introduced a compulsory academic element for the first time into art education, and in 1974 these were scrapped in favour of the BA (Hons) in Art and Design, 'effectively integrating art education into the national system of higher qualifications'. John Beck and Matthew Cornford, 'The Art School in Ruins', *Journal of Visual Culture* 11 (1) (April 2012), p. 62

37. There is a wealth of literature on the subject, particularly on the Bologna Process, which aims at harmonising the architecture of the European Higher Education system. It has been criticised for its neoliberal standardisation and emphasis on measurable outcomes. Irit Rogoff is one artworld pundit writing on this process and its potential. See Paul O'Neill and Mick Wilson, eds., *Curating and the Educational Turn* (London: Open Editions, 2010); also see http://summit.kein.org/node/191; www.artandresearch.org.uk/v2n2/lesage.html

38. Virno, *A Grammar of the Multitude.*

39. Boltanski and Chiapello, *The New Spirit of Capitalism.*

40. *Détournement,* a 'reversal of perspective' or an 'embezzlement of convention'*, is a now common activist technique, but it is important to remember that the Situationists saw themselves as an artist group in the tradition of the Lettrists, subsequently becoming increasingly political. Their reference points were art practice and art history (Dada and Surrealism) and, I will argue, it is this that makes their work art in the first place, however useful it was as a language of activism as well. *Sadie Plant, *The Most Radical Gesture: The Situationist International in a Postmodern Age* (New York and London: Routledge, 1992).

41. Michel de Certeau, *Heterologies: Discourse on the Other*, trans. Brian Massumi (Manchester: Manchester University Press, 1986).
42. The Levinasian notion of the 'unknowableness' of the Other is criticised by Grant Kester in *Conversation Pieces: Community + Communication in Modern Art (*Berkeley and London: University of California Press, 2004) because, he deduces, it models an ethical engagement based on 'mute supplication' (p. 123). His is a misreading of Levinas. Political philosopher Simon Critchley describes a Levinasian politics: '"Politics begins as ethics" means that political space is based on the irreducibility of ethical transcendence, where the community takes on meaning in difference without reducing difference. Political space is an open, plural, opaque network of ethical relations which are non-totalisable and where "the contemporaneity of the multiple is tied around the diachrony of the two". Levinasian politics is the enactment of plurality, of multiplicity.' Simon Critchley, *The Ethics of Deconstruction: Derrida and Levinas* (Edinburgh: Edinburgh University Press, 1999 [1992]), p. 225.
43. Hardt and Negri, *Empire*, pp. 203–4.
44. Michel de Certeau, *Heterologies: Discourse on the Other*, p. 207. See particularly 'The Laugh of Michel Foucault' and 'History: Science and Fiction'.
45. Gerald Raunig, *Art and Revolution.*
46. Michel de Certeau, *Heterologies: Discourse on the Other*, p. 194.

Chapter 6

1. Rancière, *Dissensus: On Politics and Aesthetics*, pp. 135–44.
2. Michel Foucault, 'On the Genealogy of Ethics', in Rabinow, ed., *The Foucault Reader*, p. 351.

Despite being elided with Lacanian theoretical positions by the artworld and Foucault's own engagement with Deleuze's theories, Foucault's understanding does not stem from the discipline of psychoanalysis. His idea of a multiple or plural self is not formulated in psychoanalytic terms. Coming frosm the discipline of philosophy, Foucault's is a Nietzschean concept of the multiplicity of selves. Nietzsche proposes this multiplicity in an 1885 note, by saying that 'the assumption of one single subject is perhaps unnecessary; perhaps it is just as permissible to assume a multiplicity of subjects, whose interaction and struggle is the basis of our thought and our consciousness in general? ... *My hypothesis:* The subject as multiplicity.' Further, Nietzsche thought that it was organisation and patterns of domination that allowed pluralities to appear as unities. Friedrich Nietzsche, *The Will to Power*, trans. Walter Kaufman and R. J. Hollingdale (New York: Vintage, 1968), pp. 270, 303.

3. Gilles Deleuze, 'Intellectuals and Power', reprinted from *L'Arc*, 49 (1972), pp. 3–10, in Buchard, ed., *Language, Counter-Memory, Practice*, pp. 205–17, p. 214.

4. For example, see Charlotte Burns, 'Newer, bigger, better? Eggleston reprints sell out', *The Art Newspaper*, Issue 234, April 2012.

5. Sánchez Vázquez, *Art and Society*, p. 82.

6. Foucault, 'On the Genealogy of Ethics', p. 351.

7. Maurizio Passerin d'Entrèves, *The Political Philosophy of Hannah Arendt* (London: Routledge, 1994), p. 141.

8. Hannah Arendt, *The Human Condition* (Chicago: University of Chicago Press, 1965 [1958]), p. 7.

Index

activism 1–3, 8–11, 27, 49, 57, 65–6, 73, 76–80, 95, 103, 107, 111–17, 120, 122, 139–50
anthropology 2, 29–30, 51, 84–6, 104, 119–30, 135–7, 158
archaeology 2, 122–3, 129–36
Arendt, Hannah 160–1
art:
education 19, 67
history 28, 47, 57, 67–8,
Institutional definition of 7–11, 43–57, 66, 71, 106, 126–7, 133, 157–8, 160
and science 51, 130–5
autonomy 59, 9 3, 97–101, 140, 159
avant-garde 26–9, 36, 42, 49, 67–8, 72–7, 97, 101, 108,

biennials 17, 21, 27–31, 37–9, 52, 58, 94, 148
Bishop, Claire 48, 50, 102–4

capitalism 15, 21, 37, 53, 80, 84, 89, 95, 102–3, 135, 138–42, 151, 153, 155
The New Spirit of 42, 72, 142
Certeau, Michel de 143–6
conceptual art 9, 36, 45, 48, 102–3
conceptualism 175
creativity 31, 46, 54, 86, 142–3

Danto, Arthur 45–50, 53–6, 95
dematerialised 35–6, 103–4
deregulation 19–22, 37–41
Dickie, George 45–7, 53–8
discipline 4, 6, 10–11, 57, 104, 112, 117–50
anti-discipline 121, 156–7
disciplinarity 119–50, 156–60
interdisciplinarity 137, 140
discourse 20, 40, 85–6, 90, 106, 119, 125–6, 128, 145–6, 157–61
artworld 19, 28, 34, 44–53, 55, 58–9, 89, 94–6, 156
neoliberal 33, 41, 69, 72, 107, 111
totalising 3, 10–11, 73–4, 148–52, 157, 159, 161
distinction 7, 58, 106

education 74–7, 121–4
evolutionary theory, Darwinian 138–9
existentialism 81–2, 89

false consciousness 65, 73–6
feminism 74–79
Foucault, Michel 7–9, 45, 66–73, 80–90, 107, 121–2, 132, 135, 146, 153–7
Freire, Paolo 76–7, 143

Greenberg, Clement 9–10, 45, 54, 93–8, 101, 121
artlike art 93, 105–9, 121, 145, 156

Hardt, Michael and Negri, Antonio 112, 145
history 57, 84–7,

art history 96–105, 119, 122–3, 132–6, 141–2, 147–50
humanism 82, 135, 154

Kant, Immanuel 67, 93–9, 105
Kaprow, Allan 9–10, 93–104, 145
lifelike art 93–113, 117, 121, 145, 148, 174, 175
knowledge 51, 66, 75–6, 77, 90, 131–2, 142–4, 146, 151, 154, 158
art as 10–11, 117, 119–40, 147–9, 160
economy 17, 21, 34–7, 103, 139–40

Latour, Bruno 51, 124–8
Levinas, Emanuel 143–4, 180
liberalisation, trade 17–19, 37–9

market 6, 8, 11, 19, 22–4, 27–9, 31–4, 38, 40–1, 45, 49–50, 53, 63, 88–9, 99, 101–11, 120–1, 140, 148, 153–5, 158–9
art 10–11, 17, 21, 26–42, 51–3, 57, 68–9, 71, 93–7, 146–9, 151–4, 160
Marxism 8, 18–19, 27, 67, 78, 82, 87, 153–5
meritocracy 21, 29, 38
Marxist:
art history 97–9
dialectics 78–80
measurement 42, 94, 105–12, 120, 153
modern:
Modernism 25–8, 38, 98–9, 103, 129, 151
modernity 3, 67, 101, 107–8, 129, 133–5, 153–9

New Labour 24, 34, 41, 70–2, 107–9
Nietzsche, Friedrich 82, 158, 173, 180–1

philosophy
of art 43–57
of history 78–80
PLATFORM 1–2, 149–50
politics 3–4, 8–9, 27, 42, 45, 49, 51–2, 58, 68–70, 79–80, 89–90, 93, 108, 111–12, 144–5, 152–3, 158–60
populism 50, 94, 110–13, 153
postmodernism 10, 67, 80, 98, 106–8, 154
privatisation 17–21, 70
mixed economy 21–6
art market 26–34
intellectual property 34–7

Rancière, Jacques 7, 9, 45, 55, 68, 75, 146, 152, 160
relational aesthetics 48–9, 52, 91, 102–4

Sartre, Jean-Paul 81–2, 89, 154
self-responsibilisation 70, 109, 153–4

teleology 79–80, 98, 138–9
Thomas, Nicholas 2, 84–6

Wittgenstein, Ludwig 45–50